And the Winner Is . . .

By Jenny Miglis
Illustrated by Caleb Meurer
Based on the teleplay Big Pink Loser by Jay Lender,
William Reiss, and Merriwether Williams

One morning Patrick received a package in the mail. It was a trophy! He could barely contain his excitement. "My very first award!" he cried with glee. "I've got to show SpongeBob!"

Patrick barreled through SpongeBob's front door. He cleared his throat and read aloud, "'For Outstanding Achievement in Achievement . . . SpongeBob SquarePants?' Huh? That's a funny way to spell my name!"

SpongeBob looked down at his feet. "Uh, Patrick, there must be some mistake," he said. "That award is for me."

"B-b-but I never won an award before," Patrick whined. "It's so shiny."
"I've got something else that's shiny in my coat closet! A button!"
said SpongeBob. "You can have it!"

"Goody! I'll get it!" Patrick cried. He flung open the door of a nearby closet. Awards and trophies of all shapes and sizes tumbled out.

"Not there!" SpongeBob cried. "That's my . . . award closet," he mumbled.

CRASH!

"Waah! I want an award!" Patrick wailed. "I'm not good at anything!"

SpongeBob wrapped his arm around Patrick's shoulder. "But you're Patrick STAR!" he exclaimed. "You can do anything you set your mind to!"

"Okay, I want to defeat the giant monkey men and save the ninth dimension!" Patrick said.

"That's too big. Something smaller," SpongeBob said.

"Defeat the little monkey men and save the eighth dimension?" Patrick asked.

SpongeBob sighed. "The smallest thing you can think of!" he said.

Patrick thought for a moment. "A job at the Krusty Krab?"

"Great idea!" said SpongeBob. "Let's go!"

"It was nice of Mr. Krabs to give me a job here. Do I get my award yet?" Patrick asked as he ate a Krabby Patty.

"You have to work for it," SpongeBob said, reminding him. "Pick up this order and take it to the customers," he instructed.

Patrick picked up the food and walked toward the table in the back. But just as he reached it he tripped, spilling Krabby Patties all over the floor.

"Good try," SpongeBob said. "But next time make sure the food actually gets to the customer."

"Why don't you answer the phone?" SpongeBob suggested.

"Aye, aye, captain!" Patrick exclaimed as the first call rang in.

"Is this the Krusty Krab?" the customer on the line asked.

"No, this is Patrick," Patrick replied and hung up.

The phone rang again. *Briiing! Briiing!*
"Hello, is this the Krusty Krab?" the second customer asked.

"NO! This is PATRICK!" Patrick hollered. "And I am NOT a crusty crab!" SpongeBob shook his head. "That's the name of the restaurant, Patrick." "Aww, fishpaste," Patrick said with a sigh. "I can't do anything right."

"Sure you can, Patrick," SpongeBob encouraged. "Uh, you can . . . you're good at . . . hmm . . ." He couldn't think of anything. "I've got it! I bet you know how to open a jar!"

SpongeBob took a jar of tartar sauce from the shelf and unscrewed the lid. "It's easy! Now you try. First, get a jar," he instructed.

Patrick rooted around in the refrigerator and emerged holding something that was clearly not a jar.

"No, Patrick, that's a pickle," SpongeBob said patiently.

After a few tries Patrick finally found a jar of jellyfish jelly.

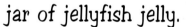

"Good. Now just do exactly as I do. Exactly," said SpongeBob as he demonstrated.

"Exactly," Patrick repeated as he slowly turned the lid until it popped off.

"Oh, no! I broke it!" Patrick cried.

"No, Patrick, you did it!" SpongeBob exclaimed. "Good job!"

"I did?" Patrick asked with disbelief. "I opened the jar with my own hand! And it was all because you showed me how to do it, SpongeBob!"

"Patrick, if you do exactly what I do you'll have an award in no time!"

The next day Patrick greeted SpongeBob outside his house.

"Wow!" SpongeBob said. "It's amazing how a simple change of clothes can make a guy look just like . . . me!" He did a double take. "Huh?"

Patrick straightened his tie. "If I'm going to be a winner, I've got to dress like one," he declared.

"Okay, Patrick, whatever you say," SpongeBob said with a shrug. "Are you ready for work? I'm ready!"

"I'm ready! I'm ready! I'm ready!" Patrick chanted.

"Oops! Forgot my hat!" SpongeBob said.

"Oops! Me too!" Patrick said.

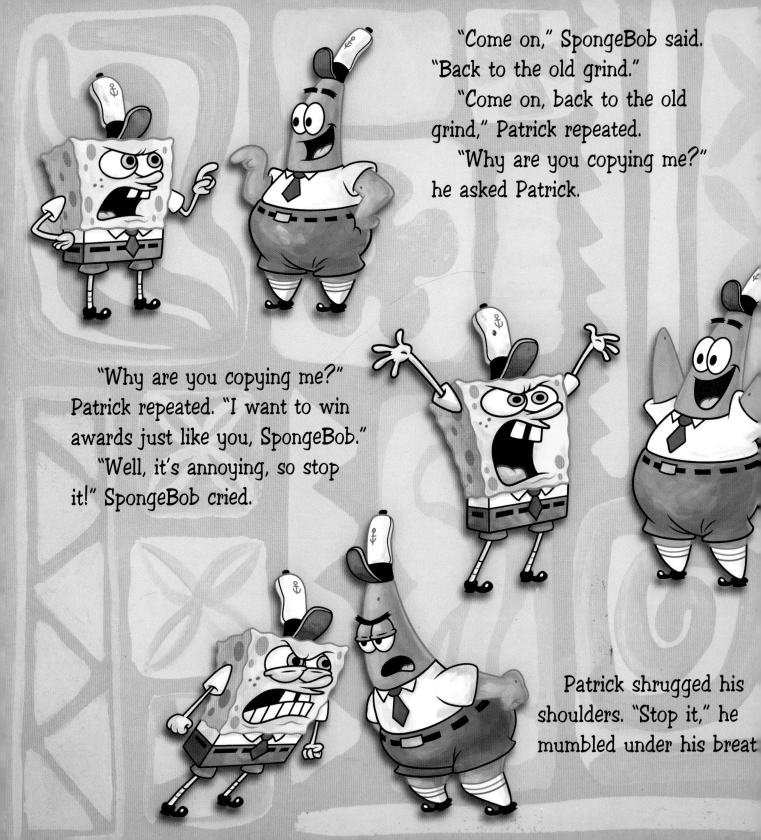

"Come on," SpongeBob said. "Back to the old grind."

"Come on, back to the old grind," Patrick repeated.

"Why are you copying me?" he asked Patrick.

"Why are you copying me?" Patrick repeated. "I want to win awards just like you, SpongeBob."

"Well, it's annoying, so stop it!" SpongeBob cried.

Patrick shrugged his shoulders. "Stop it," he mumbled under his breat

"Aaaaaagh!" SpongeBob screamed. Then he had an idea. "Hi! My name is Patrick Star!" he said. "I'm the laziest, pinkest starfish in Bikini Bottom and I wish I were ME and not SpongeBob!"

But this time Patrick didn't imitate SpongeBob. "What's so great about being a big pink nobody? I was never closer to an award than the minute I started copying you," he said and hung his head.

Just then a delivery truck pulled up.
"Trophy delivery!" the truck driver called out.
"Must be another award for SpongeBob
TrophyPants!" Patrick sneered. "What's it for thi
time, perfect squareness?"

SpongeBob took the trophy and held it up to the light. "'For Doing Absolutely Nothing Longer Than Anyone Else,'" he read, "'Patrick Star.'" SpongeBob couldn't believe his eyes. "Patrick! This trophy is for you!"

"For me?" Patrick gasped. "I always knew I'd win an award!"

"So, what are you going to do now that you've won it?" SpongeBob asked. Patrick propped himself up against the trophy. "Nothing, of course," Patrick said. "I've got to protect my title!"

CREATIVE LIVING

EASY HOME CRAFT AND DECORATING PROJECTS

CREATIVE
HOME
ARTS
CLUB

Minnetonka, Minnesota

CREATIVE LIVING
EASY HOME CRAFT AND DECORATING PROJECTS

Printed in 2006.

Published by North American Membership Group under license from International Masters Publishers, Inc.

Tom Carpenter
Creative Director

Heather Koshiol
Managing Editor

Jenya Prosmitsky
Book Design & Production

2 3 4 5 6 / 08 07 06 05
ISBN 1-58159-250-7
© 2005 Creative Home Arts Club

Creative Home Arts Club
12301 Whitewater Drive
Minnetonka, MN 55343
www.creativehomeartsclub.com

Special thanks to Terry Casey, Janice Cauley, Happi Olson and Nadine Trimble.

CONTENTS

INTRODUCTION

Welcome to
CREATIVE LIVING

Your guide to
EASY HOME CRAFT AND
DECORATING PROJECTS

For Creative Home Arts Club members like you, creativity is a way of life. With interest and skills in various crafting techniques, you're always looking for opportunities to practice and use your creative talents on a variety of projects.

And variety is just what you'll find in *Creative Living*. These *Easy Home Craft and Decorating Projects* help fulfill your urge to create. Each project's step-by-step instructions mean you don't have to figure out the best way to re-cover a chair or craft a beaded lampshade. Plus you'll discover fresh and exciting techniques like how to make your own batik fabric or construct custom display shelving.

So put your creativity to work! Sew, paint, add special finishes, decorate, build, craft or work with flowers. It's all right here.

Creative Living offers complete how-to instructions along with clear, illustrative photos to help you along the way. We've also included detailed materials lists to take away any guesswork and let you focus your creative energy on choosing the colors or patterns or textures you want for a unique look.

Get your craft area ready to begin your next project. And get ready for *Creative Living*!

CREATIVE
HOME
ARTS
—CLUB—

SEWING
PROJECTS

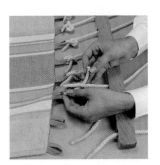

Fabric texture, color and design present you with wonderful opportunities to give your creativity a good workout. Vary your fabric selection to create the same project in very different styles—bright and fun, soft and romantic, or crisp and modern. This chapter includes ideas for pillows, throws and slipcovers ... plus simple instructions on how to create your own batik fabric. These projects, ranging from casual to elegant, will always bear your unique touch of individuality.

MAKE-IT-IN-A-WEEKEND COMFORTER

Add warmth and color to your bed with our easy-to-sew comforter.

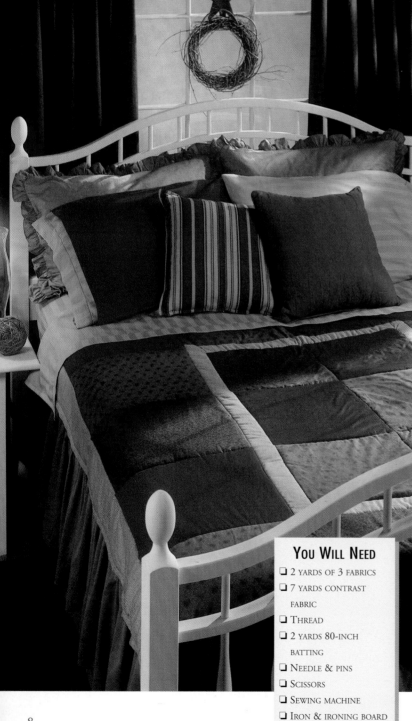

BEFORE YOU BEGIN

Use graph paper and colored pencils to work out the comforter's design before you begin cutting the fabric.

Cutting the Fabric

Once you have worked out quilt pattern and desired placement of colors, cut fabric into squares and strips as outlined below. These measurements include ½-inch seam allowances all around.
• Finished comforter is 68 by 80 inches. Cut backing fabric 69 inches wide by 81 inches long.
You will also need:
• 14 squares (each 15 by 15 inches) for all outer squares.

• 2 rectangles (each 15 by 13 inches) for J and K squares
• 4 squares (each 13 by 13 inches) for F, G, N and O squares
• 2 strips (each 3 by 25 inches) for inner horizontal strips
• 2 strips (7 by 59 inches) for outer horizontal strips
• 2 strips (7 by 83 inches) for outer vertical strips.

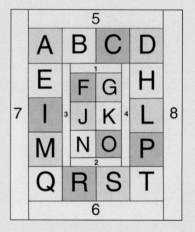

Piecing Squares and Strips

Using graph paper chart, label each square and strip with a letter or number as indicated in illustration. Then follow this stitching order:
1. Join squares AEIMQ
2. Join squares DHLPT
3. Join squares B and C, then R and S horizontally
4. Join FJN and then GKO vertically
5. Join FJN to GKO
6. Join inner horizontal strips (1 and 2) to FG and NO

7. Join inner vertical strips (3 and 4) to FJN and GKO
8. Join inner horizontal strips (1 and 2) to BC and RS to complete interior block
9. Join strips AEIMQ and DHLPT to interior block to complete comforter interior
10. Join outer horizontal strips to comforter (5 to ABCD and 6 to QRST) then vertical strips (7 to AEIMQ and 8 to DHLPT)

SEWING THE COMFORTER

1 With right sides together, join fabric squares as indicated in Before You Begin. Backstitch at beginning and end of each row to lock seams. Press seam allowances open.

2 Once six interior squares are joined, sew interior strips 1, 2, 3 and 4 in place as shown in Before You Begin. Continue, following order indicated in Before You Begin, until patchwork is complete.

3 On large work space, lay out backing piece, wrong side up. Lay batting on top of backing and patchwork on top of batting with right side up. Pin or hand baste layers together, working from center to edges.

HANDY HINTS

When joining squares of different colors, press seam allowances toward darker square to eliminate show-through if one square is much darker than another.

DOLLAR SENSE

To avoid buying too much batting, look for batting designed for quilt-making that is sold in standard quilt-sized pieces.

TAKE NOTE

If tucks or puckers appear in stitching, reduce the pressure on the machine's presser foot. An even-feed or walking foot also helps avoid this problem.

4 Set a long stitch length and loose tension on sewing machine. Beginning in center of comforter, and working toward outside edge, machine stitch through all patchwork seam lines to quilt comforter.

5 When quilting is complete, trim batting and backing to 4 inches from last quilting stitch. Press under ½ inch; fold over patchwork edge onto backing. Pin and stitch through all layers around entire comforter.

BLANKET STITCH PILLOW

Blanket stitching is a quick and fun way to finish a pillow.

BEFORE YOU BEGIN

A blanket stitch is a traditional embroidery stitch that is both functional and decorative. Use it as an attractive finish for borders and appliqués.

Pillow Pointers

For the pillow, choose a fabric with a dense weave or a nonwoven material that does not ravel. Felted wool, acrylic felt, polyester fleece, vinyl and leather are ideal for blanket stitching.

Measure the pillow form, add ½ inch to each side; cut two pieces of fabric for the pillow.

Stitch Tips

Using a dressmaker's pencil, mark a border with a line of evenly spaced dots.

To blanket stitch, work from left to right with the pillow edge facing you. For the first stitch, place the needle under the pillow front, near the edge and pull it through. Push the needle down through the first dot, out to the fabric edge and over the thread. Pull taut, positioning the thread along the fabric edge.

Repeat the process for each stitch, pulling the needle through the next penciled dot (below).

Blanket stitches are often called buttonhole stitches. While they are made in the same way, blanket stitches have more space between them than buttonhole stitches, which lie directly next to each other.

The longer the stitch, the deeper the border will be.

When blanket stitching appliqués onto fabric, start stitches at the smallest area of the design.

When stitching around corners and curves, keep the bottom of the stitches along the edge of the fabric evenly spaced (below).

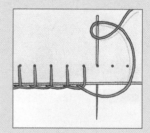

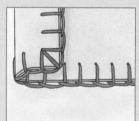

BLANKET STITCHING A PILLOW EDGE

HANDY HINTS

For blanket stitching, choose thread that contrasts with the color of the fabric. Otherwise, the decorative stitching will not stand out around the border of the pillow.

To reinforce seams, add ½ inch to all pillow sides for the seam allowances. Stitch around the pillow, then blanket stitch from the edge of the fabric up to the seam stitches.

1 With wrong sides facing, pin the pillow pieces together. Using a stitch guide and dressmaker's pencil, mark small placement dots around the pillow, ½ inch from the edge and with ½ inch between the dots.

2 Thread a crewel needle with embroidery floss and begin blanket stitching around the pillow. Use six strands of floss for a thick border, three for a delicate border. Pull the thread taut so the stitches lie flat.

3 To blanket stitch around a corner, stitch through the same top hole as the previous stitch, then anchor the stitch at the point in the corner. Stitch through the same hole again; carry the stitch to the next side.

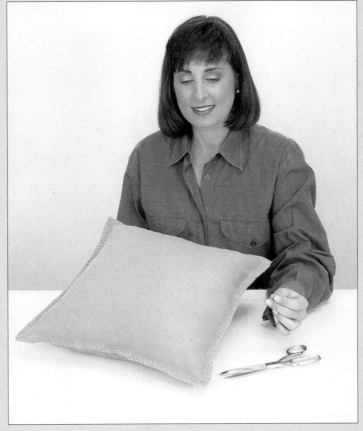

4 Before stitching across the last side, insert the pillow form into the pillow cover and pin the edges of the fabric together. Continue blanket stitching along the pinned edge of the pillow.

5 When the pillow is completely bordered with blanket stitches, secure the stitches by tying a knot in the thread, then pulling the needle between the layers of fabric to hide the thread ends. Using scissors, clip the thread close to the edges of the pillow and push the loose ends between the fabric. Fluff the pillow.

REVERSIBLE TAB-TOP CURTAINS

You can redecorate in a flash with reversible curtains.

YOU WILL NEED

- ❏ FACE FABRIC
- ❏ LINING FABRIC
- ❏ MEASURING TAPE
- ❏ METAL RULER
- ❏ MARKING PEN OR PENCIL
- ❏ SCISSORS
- ❏ THREAD & PINS
- ❏ SEWING MACHINE
- ❏ IRON & IRONING BOARD
- ❏ BUTTONS
- ❏ SEAM RIPPER

BEFORE YOU BEGIN

Decorative fabrics on the front and back panels of tab-top curtains make it easy to change the decor of a room or simply to add a second color or print to the window.

Measuring and Cutting the Fabric

Tab length = Loop measuring tape around curtain rod to position on window molding where upper edge of curtain will begin; add 2 inches.
Tab width = 5 inches.
Curtain length = Measure from end of tabs to desired length; add 1 inch.

Number of tabs = Figure the width of panel divided by 4-inch-wide tabs plus 4-inch spacing between tabs. Alter spacing as needed to fit tabs evenly across panel.
Yardage = Figure the number of panels times finished length plus ¼ yard for tabs.

Creating a Bordered Edge

For an interesting alternative, consider bringing the lining fabric around to the front of the curtain for a touch of color contrast. Cut the lining panel 9 inches wider than the face fabric to create a 4-inch border of lining on each side of each curtain panel. Pin long edges of lining and face fabrics right sides together with raw edges even; stitch. Press seams open.

Lay curtain panel flat—the lining will automatically fold over to the right side of the curtain (right). Then,

pin upper and lower edges, inserting tab ends in upper edge seam. Stitch both edges, leaving a 12-inch opening in lower edge. Turn right side out; press panel flat so lining edges appear on face side of curtain. Finish as shown in Step 5.

LINING FABRIC

FACE FABRIC

Making Tabs

Cut strips equal to tab length and width from each piece of fabric. To create point, use a ruler and marking pen to mark lines (below).

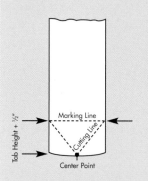

Tab Height + ½"

Marking Line

Cutting Line

Center Point

Alternatively, make narrow tabs tied in bows, which look less formal than button tabs. You will need more tabs to fill the panel evenly and to keep the curtain from drooping. Make two 18-inch-long, 2-inch-wide tabs for each tab position. Pin tabs and top edge as in Step 3. Then stitch upper and lower edges, leaving a 12-inch opening along lower edge. Turn right side out; press. Stitch opening closed. Tie tabs into square knots to hang.

SEWING THE CURTAINS

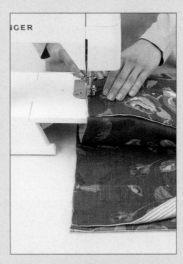

1 To form tabs, take one tab strip from each fabric. With right sides together, sew around shaped edge and both long edges with ½-inch seam allowance. Trim seam allowance; cut corners at diagonal.

2 Turn tabs right side out; press. Make vertical buttonholes in center of each tab; hole length should equal button diameter plus button thickness. Use seam ripper to cut buttonholes open; press.

3 Pin and baste tabs in place on upper edge of face fabric with raw edges even and tabs extending downward. Make sure both tabs and curtain panels have matching fabric faceup.

4 With right sides facing and tabs sandwiched between, pin lining and curtain panels together. Leave 12-inch opening on bottom. Trim seam allowance; clip corners. Turn right side out; press.

5 Hand stitch opening closed. Mark button placement on curtain. Stitch buttons to both sides of curtain to make it reversible. Button tabs and slip onto curtain rod.

ELEGANT FABRIC THROW

A fabric throw brings both elegance and comfort to any room.

BEFORE YOU BEGIN

Use the best affordable fabrics along with a good-quality fringe for an elegant and luxurious fabric throw that will last.

Different Trim Styles

Fringes and trims add a decorative touch to any fabric surface whether it's on fabric throws, pillows or slipcovers. Unify a room with matching colors and styles of trims.

Specialty cording (right) is twisted or braided with an attached lip for easy insertion into a seam.

Tassel fringe (top right) features hanging tufts of yarn along a heading. The heading can be inserted in a seam or stitched onto the surface of the fabric.

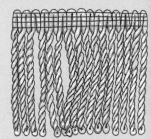

Bullion fringe (center right) is a long, twisted fringe that's popular among decorators. It can be found in a rainbow of colors and a variety of lengths.

Ribbons and braids, available in endless varieties, are used for their decorative appeal on the surface of a fabric treatment. Use ribbons and braids (above) to cover a seam or add color and texture.

Trim Methods

A fringe trim adds a designer touch to the edge of any throw.
• Keep a fabric swatch on hand when purchasing fringe to ensure that color, weight and texture work together.

• Most fringes have a flexible heading that can be stitched or glued to fabric. Some fringes can be fused into position with a self-adhesive heading.

MAKING A FABRIC THROW

1 Cut both fabric pieces to desired size. Decide which fabric will be right side of throw. Pin pieces with right sides facing. Stitch all sides, pivoting at corners and leaving a 12-inch opening along one side.

2 Clip corners diagonally to reduce bulk. Trim and grade seams, keeping the seam allowance of the face fabric the widest. Turn throw right side out; press. Slipstitch opening closed.

3 Apply seam sealant to cut edges of trim to prevent fraying. Turn under ¼ inch on each end of trim. Starting along the bottom edge, pin bullion trim around all edges, easing fullness around corners.

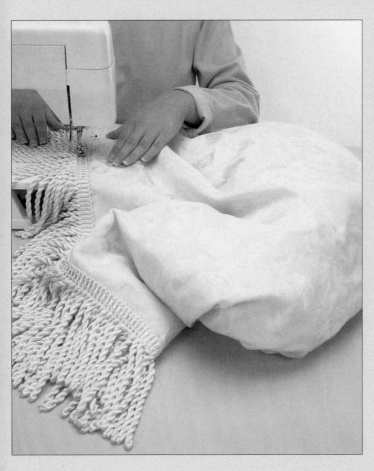

4 Folded ends of trim should meet with no gap. Patterns or designs on heading should line up. Topstitch fringe in place with two rows of stitching, using matching threads.

Ottoman Slipcover

An attractive slipcover breathes new life into a plain ottoman.

YOU WILL NEED
- ❏ OTTOMAN
- ❏ DECORATIVE FABRIC
- ❏ DECORATIVE TRIM
- ❏ NEWSPRINT
- ❏ TAPE MEASURE
- ❏ SEWING MACHINE
- ❏ NEEDLE & THREAD
- ❏ ELASTIC
- ❏ LARGE SAFETY PIN
- ❏ IRON

BEFORE YOU BEGIN

A premade pattern makes it easier to match stripes, plaids and floral repeats.

Measuring and Cutting the Fabric

Using your ottoman as a guide, make a custom pattern from newsprint.

• Measure and cut a pattern for the top equal to the ottoman length (A) by width (B), plus 3 inches on each side.

• Make a pattern for the skirt equal to the ottoman height (C) plus 2½ inches for hem and seams by length (A), plus width (B), plus 1 inch for seams.

• Pin the pattern to the fabric. Cut one top piece and two skirt pieces. Also cut, for the elastic casing, 2-inch-wide strips; piece them together to equal the circumference of the ottoman, plus 1 inch.

• Cut the decorative trim to the circumference, plus 1 inch, and the 1-inch-wide elastic to the circumference, less 1 inch.

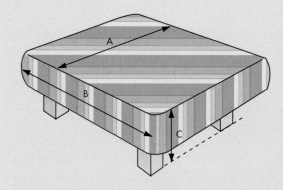

Creating the Skirt

Piece the skirt together. With right sides facing and raw edges aligned, stitch short sides of skirt together to form continuous band. Press seams open. Press bottom edge under ½ inch, then 1½ inches for hem.

STITCHING AN OTTOMAN SLIPCOVER

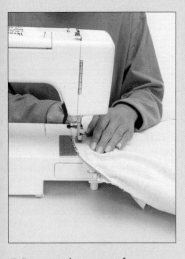

1 From each corner of top piece (Before You Begin), trim 1 inch diagonally. With right sides facing and raw edges aligned, stitch skirt around ottoman top, easing skirt to fit at corners. Trim seams.

2 Fold long sides of fabric for elastic casing under ½ inch to wrong side of fabric and press. Raw edges of fabric should meet at center. Fold short sides of strip under ½ inch and press.

3 Pin casing to wrong side of slipcover so one long side is aligned with seam line and other long side falls against top. Stitch casing in place on both sides. Leave short sides open.

HANDY HINTS

For an ottoman with designer style, cut the top of the slipcover from one fabric and the skirt from a different but coordinating fabric. Tie the look together with a trim that matches both pieces of fabric.

DOLLAR SENSE

Upscale upholstery trims can be expensive. To make your own at a fraction of the cost, cover thick cording with fabric that contrasts the slipcover fabric.

Because little fabric is needed for slipcovers, you can often use remnants and smaller yardages of fine fabrics found in discount bins.

4 Beginning at one corner on right side of skirt, position and pin decorative trim around slipcover following seam line. Overlap trim ends where they meet, then topstitch in place using matching thread.

5 Attach a large safety pin to end of elastic, then begin threading pin and elastic through one short side of casing. Continue until entire piece of elastic has been threaded through casing.

6 Pull elastic through casing, then stitch ends of elastic together to secure. Slipstitch casing closed. Press slipcover with warm iron, then position over ottoman, matching corners. Adjust gathers evenly around ottoman or as desired.

SIMPLE BATIK FABRIC

Create a unique form of fabric decoration with the art of batik.

YOU WILL NEED

❑ FABRIC
❑ DRESSMAKER'S CARBON
   & TRACING WHEEL
❑ BATIK WAX
❑ DOUBLE BOILER & WAX
   THERMOMETER
❑ BATIK FRAME OR
   CANVAS STRETCHER
❑ PUSH PINS
❑ FABRIC DYES & BASIN
❑ SMALL, STIFF-BRISTLE
   PAINTBRUSH
❑ DULL KNIFE
❑ IRON & IRONING BOARD
❑ NEWSPRINT

BEFORE YOU BEGIN

All batik begins with planning a pattern. Whether the design is a random application of colors or a specific motif, the layers of color must be thought out ahead of time.

Preparing to Batik

Plan design and coordinate color scheme on paper. Use crayons or colored markers to color paper pattern; use for reference.

When planning colors, also plan the dyeing sequence. Start with lightest colors and work up to the darkest. Remember how colors combine. For example, fabric dyed yellow and then blue will turn a shade of green. Also consider the color of your fabric. Anything other than white or cream fabrics will affect the dye color. Once fabric is dry, paint with wax any areas meant to remain the color of the first dye.

Use a photocopier to enlarge template (below) of sun-flower to desired size. Transfer design to fabric with dressmaker's carbon and tracing wheel, or use an air-soluble fabric marking pen. The color of carbon paper should contrast with fabric but remain visible after dyeing.

To make a simple pillow from fabric, cut same size of fabric for back. With right sides facing, sew front to back, leaving an opening. Trim corners and turn right side out. Insert pillow form in opening, slipstitch opening closed.

To add ruffle, stitch gathered trim to right side of batik piece before sewing it to back piece.

Special Tools

Although the batik craft does not require special tools, some tools will simplify the process.
• A tjanting resembles a drawing pen with a reservoir that holds wax and distributes it in long flowing lines or intricate designs.
• A batik wax pot keeps the wax temperature just right (270°). But, a double boiler and wax thermometer can be substituted.

BATIK DYEING THE FABRIC

1 Transfer design to ironed and prewashed fabric. Use push pins to position fabric on batik frame or canvas stretcher, or lay it over wax paper. Heat wax to watery consistency. Paint wax on outline of pattern.

2 Once wax is hard and dry, crumple fabric to create "veining" look. Submerge cloth in yellow dye bath for about 30 minutes or until desired color. Stir to help dye penetrate fabric evenly. Rinse in cool water.

3 Once fabric has dried, paint wax onto all areas that will remain yellow. Submerge fabric in green dye bath. Wax all areas that will remain light green, such as outer leaves and center; dip cloth in green dye a second time. Rinse.

HANDY HINTS

Practice batik on small projects before attempting a large, multicolored batik.

If the fabric still has wax after ironing, use a cleaning solvent to remove small areas of leftover wax.

TAKE NOTE

Cotton is an ideal fabric for batik since it dyes well. Smooth silk is another choice; avoid raw or textured silk with irregular weaves. Avoid synthetic fabrics.

For dyes to remain true, use white fabric. When using pastel or gray fabric, the color of the dye will be affected. Make a test strip and dye each successive color over the preceding color.

4 Once cloth has dried, scrape off wax with dull knife or paint scraper. Iron off any remaining wax by placing batik between several layers of newsprint or other absorbent paper and press over papers. Continue pressing until all wax is removed.

SIMPLE SWAG

Turn a simple fabric panel into an elegant window treatment.

20

BEFORE YOU BEGIN

Because the linings of swags are visible, here is a great opportunity to mix prints and colors.

Making the Pattern

The width of this treatment equals the width of the fabric as it comes from the bolt. You only have to add the lengths of the three pattern pieces to determine how much yardage to buy.

First, mark where swag holders will be positioned. Measure from marking to marking (A); add 11 inches. Add to this amount twice the distance from swag holder to desired hem placement (B) plus 1 inch (the length is doubled to account for both hanging side pieces).

To determine how much fabric and lining you'll need to purchase, convert the total length from inches to feet. (Divide number of inches by 12 to get yardage.)

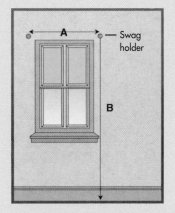

Cutting the Patterns

Cut 1 swag from both lining and face fabrics.
- Mark fabric (below) with A and A + 11 inches at selvages. A is distance between swag holders plus 1 inch.
- C is the width of the fabric or up to the width measurement plus 1 inch.
- Cut fabric along marked lines.

Cut two hanging side pieces from face fabric.
- Mark fabric (below) making pieces mirror images of each other. B is hanging side length + 1 inch and should be measured along selvage edge of fabric.
- Make side D 10 to 15 inches long, depending on how long the sides will hang.
- Cut along marked lines; repeat for lining.

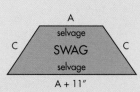

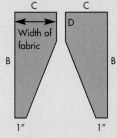

HANGING SIDES

SEWING A SWAG WITH HANGING SIDES

1 With right sides facing, sew swag to hanging sides along edge C with swag corner AC at side piece corner CD. Swag edge C may be up to 1 inch wider than side piece C. If so, ease swag to fit, so raw edges of pieces are even.

2 Repeat Step 1 with lining pieces. Then pin lining to face fabric, right sides together. Stitch, leaving a 12-inch opening on one side. Clip corners. Turn right side out; press. Hand sew opening closed.

3 Pin decorative fringe to lower edge of swag between seams with hanging sides. Turn under ½ inch of fringe at each end; stitch. Machine stitch through fringe heading and swag ½ inch from finished edge.

4 Along swag/side piece seams for face and lining, use seam ripper to cut 1-inch breaks into stitches every 4 inches to create holes for swag holder to fit through.

5 To hang swags, channel swag holder through stitch openings in seams. Start with lower edge and loop entire seam onto swag holder, ending with upper edge.

6 Mount swag holders on wall in predetermined location with necessary tools. Adjust swag folds at swag holder and drape of hanging sides until satisfied with look of window treatment.

Easy-Sew Hammock

Sew a hammock from a favorite fabric for easy relaxing all year.

BEFORE YOU BEGIN

Make a comfortable hammock using simple-to-cut fabric pieces and basic sewing skills. Choose a tightly woven, heavyweight fabric for the best support.

Hammock Variations

Consider a few variations on designing a hammock:

Create a handsome border by cutting the same striped fabric horizontally instead of vertically. Miter the border corners for a professional-looking finish. Use a single piece of fabric for the back.

Heighten border interest with edging fashioned from a complementary pattern. Make the edging narrow for a delicate accent, or very wide for assertive definition.

Cozy up the setting and enhance relaxation with a matching pillow. Cut the fabric on the bias for contrast. Sew tab ties to the corners to attach the pillow to the frame. As an option, use different fabrics on the front and back of the pillow for reversible versatility.

Measuring and Cutting

• Use medium-weight to heavyweight decorator fabrics with a tight weave for making a hammock.
• Determine the finished length and width of the hammock, using the original rope hammock as a pattern guide.
• Add ½ inch all around for seam allowances and cut two pieces of fabric to these dimensions.
• If hammock is wider than fabric panel, add equal-sized pieces to sides of center.
• Remember to plan for seam allowances when adding a contrasting border of any width.
• Add at least ¼ yard of fabric for making tabs.

SEWING A HAMMOCK

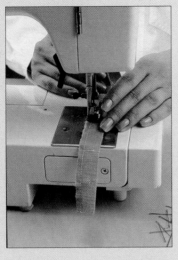

HANDY HINTS

It's a good idea to reinforce the tabs with an extra line of stitching before turning the fabric right side out.

As an alternative to tabs, substitute heavy-duty grommets (available at marine supply stores). Reinforce the heading with stiff interfacing and apply the grommets according to manufacturer's instructions.

1 Determine how many tabs you will need and mark the spacing evenly across the top and bottom width of the hammock's main piece. This finished hammock has 22 tabs on each end, spaced 2 inches apart.

2 For the tabs, cut long strips 1 inch wide. Fold each strip lengthwise, right sides together, and stitch with a ¼-inch seam. Turn strip right side out using a safety pin; press. Cut strip into as many 4-inch lengths as needed.

3 Fold each tab in half lengthwise to form a loop; pin the tabs to the hammock top at the marked spots. Loops should face toward the center of the hammock, with all raw edges even.

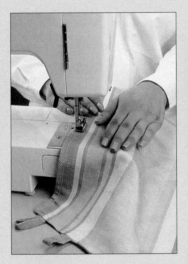

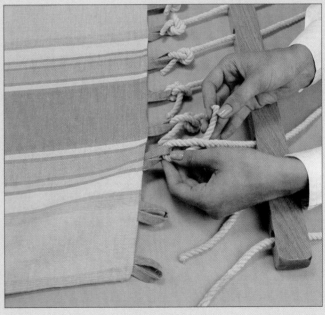

4 Pin the facing to the top fabric, right sides together. Sew around all four sides with a ½-inch seam allowance, leaving an opening on one side for turning. Trim the corners and grade the seams; turn right side out. Slipstitch the opening closed and press the entire hammock.

5 Topstitch around the hammock ¼ inch from the edge, with either plain or decorative stitching and matching or contrasting thread. Press the hammock again.

6 To fasten the hammock to the rope support system, insert the lengths of rope through the drilled wood and knot evenly and securely around each tab. Remember that the weight of a person will cause the hammock to sag closer to the floor, so adjust the knots accordingly. Hang the hammock onto the frame. Toss on a couple of throw pillows for a little extra comfort.

EASY-SEW
TAB-TIED PILLOWS

*Let colorful liners peek out from beneath
these pretty covers.*

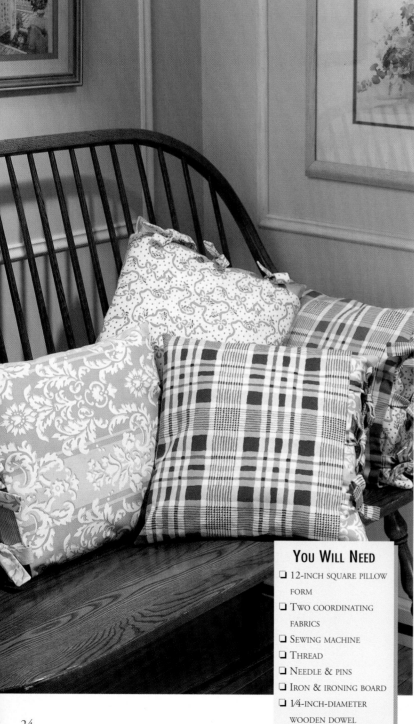

BEFORE YOU BEGIN

*With a complementary cover and tabs that tie on
one side, these tab-tied pillows transform an
ordinary square pillow into a unique decorating
accessory.*

Choosing Fabrics

• For the inner and outer
pillow covers, select patterned fabrics that share one
or more color, or that feature colors within the same
family.
• Tabs made of heavy fabrics
are harder to turn right side
out. Cottons, broadcloths,
chintz and ginghams are
ideal.
• The outside cover of the
pillow will hold its shape
better if it is made from
cotton, damask or linen,
rather than silk or rayon.

Cutting Fabric and Turning Tabs

• To cover one pillow, you
will need the following fabrics: for the inside pillow
cover, cut two 14-inch
square pieces of fabric. For
the outside pillow cover, cut
two 15- by 14½-inch pieces
and two facing strips, 15 by
3½ inches. For tab-ties, cut
12 strips, each 1¼- by 12-
inches.
• Because the tab-ties draw
attention to the pillow's
design, each tab should feature clean, straight sides and
sharp corners.

• Reinforce each corner of
the tab by stitching over the
seam twice. Be sure to clip
the corners diagonally, and
trim seams if needed.
• To turn the tab, use a
wooden dowel that fits
comfortably inside. Insert
the dowel into the short
seam edge and gently pull
the fabric over the tab
(below).
• To define each corner of
the tab, carefully pull
threads out with a pin without tearing threads.

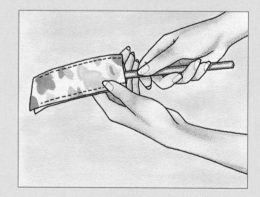

SEWING THE PILLOW COVERS

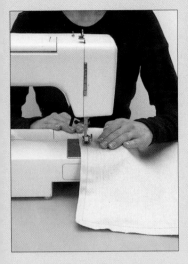  

HANDY HINTS

When using patterned fabrics, position the fabric so that the pattern falls in the center of the square. Repeat for other side.

1 With right sides facing, pin front and back panels of inside cover. Stitch ½ inch from edges; leave gap for pillow. Trim seam allowances; clip corners. Turn right side out. Insert pillow; slipstitch opening closed.

2 With right sides facing, pin two tabs on top of each other. Stitch a ¼-inch seam on three sides, leaving one short side open (Before You Begin). Turn right side out; press flat. Repeat with remaining tabs.

3 With right sides facing, pin front and back panels of outer cover. Machine stitch ½ inch from edges, leaving a 14½-inch side open. Trim seams; clip corners diagonally. Press seams open. Set aside until Step 5.

4 With right sides facing, pin two facing pieces together. Machine stitch short sides of facing together, ½ inch from edges, to form a tube. Turn one raw edge under ½ inch then ½ inch again; topstitch in place.

5 Pin three tabs to raw edge of facing. Match remaining tabs on other side of facing. Pin facing and outer pillow cover edges right sides together. Machine stitch seam ½ inch from edge, catching tabs in seam.

6 Trim seam, then turn facing to inside of cover. Press seam flat. Insert inside pillow, then tie tabs together so that inside pillow peeks through.

DAY BED SLIPCOVER

A pretty slipcover conceals utilitarian sleeping arrangements.

BEFORE YOU BEGIN

Cut paper patterns of five rectangular pieces for the cover. When cutting the fabric, take care to match the stripes in the front panels to the stripes on the top.

Measuring and Cutting

Measure the width, length and depth of the day bed mattress as well as the drop (distance from the top of the mattress to the floor).
• Cut one A rectangle equal to the dimensions of the mattress top plus ½-inch seam allowances all around.
• For panels B, C, D and E, add ½ inch to the top for seam allowances and 1 inch to the bottoms and sides for hems.
• Cut two B rectangles, each the width and depth of the mattress's short side.
• Cut two C rectangles, each the width and depth of the mattress's long side.
• Cut two D rectangles, each the width and depth of the drop on the short side.
• Cut two E rectangles the width and depth of the drop on the long side.
• For the corner ties, cut 12 rectangular pieces each measuring 3 inches by 18 inches.
• Make enough welting (below) to extend around the entire perimeter of the mattress, plus extra length to ease around the corners and overlap ends.

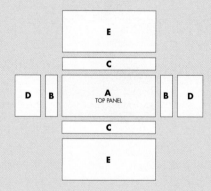

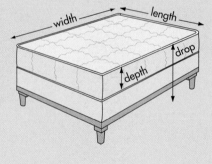

Making Welting

To make your own strips of welting, cut 2-inch-wide strips on the bias from matching or coordinating fabric. Join the short ends of the pieces with diagonal seams. Fold the strip in half lengthwise, wrong sides together. Wrap the strip around a length of cording and stitch, using a zipper foot, close to the cording.

SEWING A COVER FOR A DAY BED

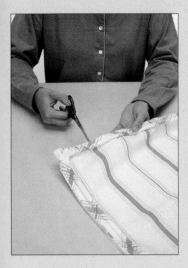

1 Pin the welting to panel A, with the cording towards the center and aligning the welting seam ½ inch from the fabric raw edges. Using a zipper foot, stitch close to the cording. Clip at the corners to ease turns.

2 On the bottom and the sides of each remaining panel, fold, press, pin and sew a double-fold ½-inch hem. To assemble the cover, pin both B panels to the top (A), right sides together and raw edges even.

3 Pin both C panels to the top (A), right sides together and raw edges aligned. Panel C will overlap the fabric of panel B, but take care not to catch the edge of panel B in the seam of panel C and vice versa.

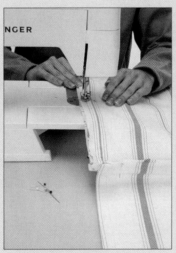

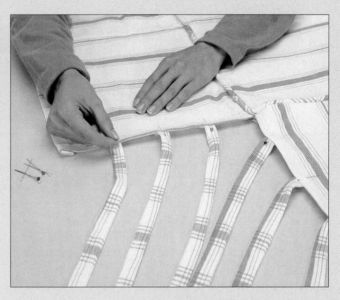

4 Pin the right sides of the D and E panels to the back of B and C, matching raw edges and removing the bottom layer of pins. Again, be careful not to catch the edges of adjacent panels in the seams.

5 Using a zipper foot, stitch through all layers close to the welting to attach the short overskirt and the longer underskirt to the top of the day bed cover. Be careful not to catch the cording in the seam.

6 To make the tabs, fold each strip in half lengthwise, wrong sides together, and sew with a ½-inch seam. Turn right side out and press. Pin pairs of tabs to the short top skirt (concealing the tops of the tabs at the back of the fabric), aligning them so they can tie neatly in the front.

PAINTING
& FINISHING
PROJECTS

Use painting and finishing techniques from this chapter to take your home decorating to a new level of creativity. These hands-on projects show you how to add depth, dimension and design to walls and surfaces including tables, chairs and floors. You choose the colors, you create the textures, you select the patterns ... then use these projects and instructions to personalize your home with your own distinct treatments.

PAINTED STRIPED WALLS

Pastel stripes in three widths add depth to walls.

YOU WILL NEED

- ❏ PLUMB LINE
- ❏ PAINTER'S MASKING TAPE
- ❏ STEEL RULER
- ❏ CARPENTER'S LEVEL
- ❏ PENCIL
- ❏ PAINT ROLLERS
- ❏ LATEX PAINTS

BEFORE YOU BEGIN

Achieve straight, perfectly vertical lines with the aid of painter's masking tape. Before applying the tape, paint the entire wall with the first of the three colors and allow to dry thoroughly overnight.

Masking the Area

Painter's tape, a low adhesive masking tape, is made especially for painting tasks. When it is removed, it does not leave a residue behind on the painted surface. Available at paint stores, this tape is conventionally blue in color and comes in several standard sizes from ¾ inch to 3 inches in width.

The width of the tape placed on the wall will be the width of the base color stripe. To create wider stripes, lay various combinations of any two tapes side by side.

Be careful not to tear or wrinkle any section while applying tape, as an imperfect edge can lead to paint bleeding.

For the neatest and quickest results, get a friend to help lay the tape along the stripe placement markings on the painted wall.

When planning stripes of different widths, prepare a layout on paper of how the stripes will repeat on the wall and around the corner (below).

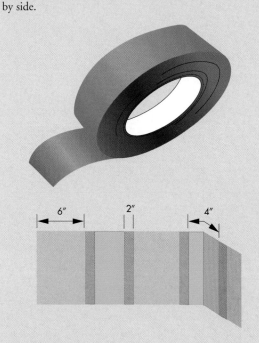

Mark Stripes

- On a base coat, drop a plumb line at the left corner of the wall. Mark the spacing for the vertical stripe at several points; connect the points using a carpenter's level as your straightedge. From this line, measure the width of each succeeding stripe.
- Mark the verticals and apply masking tape to each base coat stripe.
- Use a plumb line to check the accuracy of the stripes and adjust as needed.

PREPARING AND PAINTING THE STRIPES

1 Apply the first latex paint to the entire wall. For maximum ease of application, lay the paint on with a roller in steady motions. Allow it to dry thoroughly. This fast-drying, pink latex paint is ready in five hours.

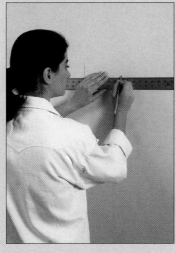

2 Starting at the plumb line (Before You Begin), measure the intervals between stripes; mark the wall at several heights. Using the marks, draw a series of floor-to-ceiling verticals as masking tape guides.

3 Lay the tape slowly and carefully along the line, starting from the bottom and unrolling it as needed. Be sure the tape adheres completely on each edge to ensure that no paint seeps underneath it later.

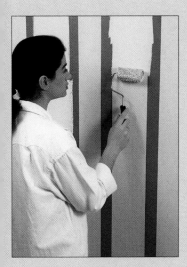

4 When the taping is all finished, apply the second color with a roller. Rollers come in many sizes and make the work go fast. Choose rollers in widths that fit the scale of the stripes being painted.

5 With a fresh roller, apply the third stripe color; in this case the pastel green. Leave the tape in place until the colors are nearly dry, up to an hour. Carefully remove the tape to avoid chipping or smearing.

CREATIVELY PAINTED STAIRCASES

Transform your plain staircase into an eye-catching focal point.

YOU WILL NEED
- ❏ LATEX PAINT
- ❏ FOAM BRUSHES
- ❏ ⅛-INCH-WIDE & 1-INCH-WIDE MASKING TAPE
- ❏ CLEAN DAMP CLOTH
- ❏ DROP CLOTH
- ❏ SANDPAPER
- ❏ TACK CLOTH

BEFORE YOU BEGIN

Before painting, protect the stair treads near the balusters by covering them with blue painter's masking tape. Press the tape firmly in place with your fingers to secure.

Prep Work for Painting

Sand the balusters and the stringer with fine-grade sandpaper; wipe clean with a tack cloth. This helps the paint adhere to the surfaces.

If there is not a visible stringer, create the effect of one by taping a diagonal line parallel to the staircase, about 5 inches from the stair treads; paint within this line.

A water-based, latex enamel paint is ideal to work with because you can wipe away any mistakes with a damp cloth. When dry, it also allows you to wipe dirt away from the painted surface.

For added interest, carry the design or pattern from the stringer onto the baluster (below left). Or, stencil a design that connects along the stringer. Here (below right), the elephant trunks connect for a festive look.

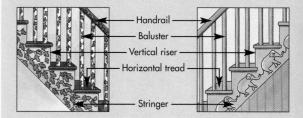

Handrail
Baluster
Vertical riser
Horizontal tread
Stringer

Design Ideas

• Repeating the designs and motifs found in rugs, upholstery and window treatment fabric is ideal for decorating the staircase.
• Cut designs from scraps of wallpaper and glue them randomly to the staircase.

• Finger paint free-form designs onto the staircase for a primitive accent.
• Combine a variety of painting techniques, such as the faux finishes of sponging and combing, to create a textured effect.

PAINTING A STAIRCASE

1 After preparing all surfaces to be painted (Before You Begin), use a small sponge brush to paint the balusters. Brush the paint vertically onto the balusters, keeping the strokes long and even. Let dry, then apply as many coats as needed to cover the wood.

2 With a wide sponge brush, paint the stringer of the staircase. Be careful to keep paint off the lower wall. If needed, wipe away any drips with a clean, damp cloth. Apply as many coats as needed. Allow to dry.

3 Using ⅛-inch-wide masking tape, divide the stringer into 3-inch sections to create a diamond pattern. Position the tape perpendicular to the edge of the stringer, using the balusters as guides. Press tape in place.

5 When the paint is dry, remove the masking tape. With a fine or medium grade of sandpaper, sand over the entire painted area. This will give the design a worn, whitewashed look. Wipe the wall clean with a damp cloth.

4 Using a 1½-inch sponge brush, paint alternate diamonds in the pattern with blue paint. Cover each diamond, being careful to keep the paint within the lines of the shape. Wipe away mistakes with a damp cloth.

PAINTED PLASTIC SHOWER CURTAIN

Brighten up a bathroom with a hand-painted shower curtain.

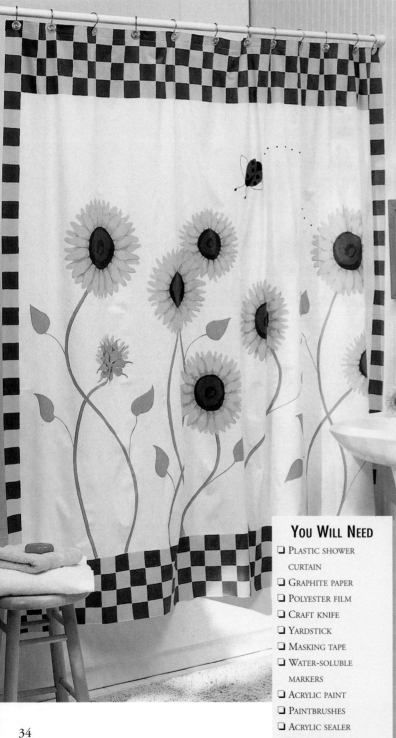

YOU WILL NEED

- ❏ PLASTIC SHOWER CURTAIN
- ❏ GRAPHITE PAPER
- ❏ POLYESTER FILM
- ❏ CRAFT KNIFE
- ❏ YARDSTICK
- ❏ MASKING TAPE
- ❏ WATER-SOLUBLE MARKERS
- ❏ ACRYLIC PAINT
- ❏ PAINTBRUSHES
- ❏ ACRYLIC SEALER

BEFORE YOU BEGIN

Painting designs on shower curtains allows unlimited decorating options. Make the curtain design a bold focal point or create a pattern that coordinates with other elements in the room.

Design Preparation

When selecting designs, keep in mind how the design will be used on the shower curtain. Make a scale drawing of the finished design to be sure the drawing fits into the curtain dimensions.

Make a checkerboard stencil of 2-inch squares for the border. Paint the border area yellow, then stencil brown squares over it. Alternatively, use a long ruler to draw a grid of 2-inch squares.

Use these templates (below) to create a sunflower garden design for your shower curtain. Simply enlarge or reduce the templates to the desired size using a photocopier, or use graph paper to draw them to scale.

Make separate templates for each color in a design element. For the sunflower, use the petal template twice. Turn the second template layer slightly off register from the first to give the illusion of layers of flower petals.

Design Plan

To make templates, place graphite paper behind the design and trace each color element of the design onto separate pieces of polyester film or poster board. Cut out with craft knife or scissors.

Paint designs onto the curtain by layering the templates. Work from the center of the design out, starting with the flower center. Line up (register) each template layer with the previous one.

PAINTING THE SHOWER CURTAIN

1 Paint border and allow to dry (Before You Begin). Using yardstick, determine placement of design elements. Roughly mark design placement positions, based on scaled design. Starting in center of curtain, tape first template layer in place.

2 Trace first template of each flower and leaf with water-soluble marker. Using acrylic paints, paint inside each outline. Working in quarter sections, move across curtain, filling in design.

3 Let paint dry thoroughly before continuing. Following design order, line up each succeeding template over previously painted design. To facilitate drying, place portable fan on work surface.

HANDY HINTS

For best results, apply a second coat of paint. Be sure to distribute the paint evenly.

TAKE NOTE

Before painting, remove creases from a folded shower curtain with a hair dryer. Clamp one end of the curtain to a work surface and stretch it with your hand while applying heat. If you can withstand the heat, the plastic will not melt.

4 After all designs are completely dry, add shading to create depth. Then, fill in free-form design details such as leaf veins, dots in flower centers and ladybugs. Seal design with acrylic sealer to protect and add longer life to design.

BLACKBOARD KITCHEN CABINETS

Blackboard paint turns cabinet doors into useful message centers.

YOU WILL NEED

- ❏ CABINET DOORS
- ❏ SANDPAPER
- ❏ CLEAN CLOTH
- ❏ PRIMER
- ❏ LATEX PAINT
- ❏ LATEX GLAZE
- ❏ SPONGE BRUSH
- ❏ PAINTER'S MASKING TAPE
- ❏ BLACKBOARD SPRAY
  PAINT
- ❏ CHALK

BEFORE YOU BEGIN

Before painting a surface with blackboard spray paint, pinpoint areas in your home that could benefit from the decorative and functional aspects of a blackboard.

Furniture Makeovers

Replace paper trails with built-in writing and drawing areas by spray painting furniture doors and walls.

Add personality to shelving units by converting cabinets into blackboards (right).

Create a blackboard surface below the chair rail in a child's room or on the front drawers of a bureau for a creative drawing center.

Paint kitchen cabinet doors to record "to do" lists, phone messages and recipes.

New Ways to Use Blackboards

An alternative to painting an existing cabinet door is to make a blackboard to the desired size from plywood; hang where needed.

Spray paint a piece of plywood with a few coats of blackboard spray. For a finishing touch, miter four pieces of wood molding and, using wood glue, secure them around the painted plywood to create a frame.

Hang the blackboard over the sofa in a family room or playroom to showcase children's art (below).

Hang a smaller blackboard on an office door to record daily appointments.

PAINTING BLACKBOARD DOORS

1 With a medium grade of sandpaper, sand the door smooth. Wipe clean, then coat the door with primer. Add a second coat if the wood grain still shows through; let dry. Sand smooth and wipe clean.

2 Use painter's masking tape to cover the section of the cabinet door to be sprayed with blackboard paint. Using a sponge brush and a dark shade of paint, paint the exposed surface of the cabinet door.

3 When dry, mix one part of paint in a lighter shade with one part of latex glaze. Working in one section at a time, paint the glaze mixture on the door, then dab away as much glaze as desired with a clean, dry cloth.

4 When dry, remove the tape from the door, then retape over the painted surface. Press the tape into the recessed area of the door. If needed, sand the primed area once again to ensure the surface is smooth.

5 Working in a well-ventilated area, apply a thin coat of spray paint over the primed surface; let dry. Lightly sand the surface to remove bubbles, then wipe with a clean cloth. Repeat as necessary to cover the door.

6 When the blackboard surface has dried completely, carefully remove all masking tape from the cabinet door. Roll a large piece of chalk on its side to cover the entire blackboard area with chalk. Rub off with a damp rag. This helps to set the surface for writing. Screw in all knobs and reattach the hinges to the door, then reposition the door on the front of the cabinet and secure.

PAINTED FAUX WOOD GRAIN

Enhance wood furniture with a painted wood graining effect.

YOU WILL NEED

❏ WOOD FURNITURE
❏ SANDPAPER
❏ CLEAN CLOTH
❏ LATEX PAINT
❏ SPONGE BRUSH
❏ LIQUID GLAZE
❏ GRAINING HEEL
❏ NON-YELLOWING
   POLYURETHANE

BEFORE YOU BEGIN

Faux wood grains can be applied in different color combinations to unfinished furniture or furniture that has already been painted. In either case, begin with a clean, sanded surface.

Preparing the Surface

For furniture that is already painted, use a rough-grade sandpaper to remove loose paint from the wood. Wipe it clean with a damp rag, then finish the furniture with a fine-grade sandpaper to smooth the surface. If the base coat will be lighter than the original color, prime the surface first.

When preparing the surface on unfinished furniture, sand the wood with fine-grade sandpaper, then wipe the dust off with a clean cloth. Apply one coat of primer before painting.

Color Combos

Faux wood graining, the simulation of natural woods, became popular during the 18th and 19th centuries. The colors traditionally used are those found in the wood, ranging from bright golden yellow to deep reddish brown to imitate expensive woods that were difficult to obtain.

For a fun twist, defy convention by using bright colors to create a style that fits your decor.

Use colors that contrast such as red and green or yellow and blue to produce some very dramatic results.

Paint Pointers

A top coat combination of paint and glaze allows the color to blend subtly with the base coat. This also gives the wood grain pattern a realistic and translucent look.

Apply an even coat of paint in lengthwise sections. A thin coat of paint will produce an indistinguishable wood grain, while a thick coat of paint will smudge and mar the lines of the grain.

CREATING A FAUX WOOD GRAIN

1 Prepare all surfaces as described in Before You Begin. Using a sponge brush, apply a base coat of latex paint to the wood; let dry and add a second coat. The brighter and heavier the base coat, the more it will show through.

2 Mix equal parts of the second color with glaze. Apply the mix to the full length of the surface area you are working on, because the graining tool cannot be stopped mid-way.

3 Beginning at one end, drag the graining heel along the surface, rocking gently to create knots in the wood grain pattern. Continue by working the design lengthwise across the surface.

HANDY HINTS

Before painting the furniture, practice rolling the graining heel on a flat surface. Drag in a lengthwise direction, rocking the heel forward and backward to create knots in the grain.

OOPS

If you make a mistake while rolling the graining heel, reapply the top coat of paint and start over. Some mistakes will make the grain appear more natural.

Once the top coat is dry, fill in areas where the paint is too thin by brushing on paint with a fine-tipped paintbrush.

4 When the design is completely dry, apply a protective coat of non-yellowing polyurethane to the surface. Allow furniture to dry. A matte finish will make the wood grain appear flat, while a shiny finish will visually lift the grain from the wood.

FESTIVE CHAIRS

Revitalize flea market chairs by painting them with fun designs.

YOU WILL NEED
- ❏ OAKTAG & CRAFT KNIFE
- ❏ WOODEN CHAIR
- ❏ CHEMICAL STRIPPER
- ❏ WOOD GLUE
- ❏ WOOD PUTTY & KNIFE
- ❏ SANDPAPER
- ❏ TACK CLOTH
- ❏ LATEX PAINTS
- ❏ PAINTBRUSHES
- ❏ MARKING PENCIL
- ❏ STENCIL BRUSH
- ❏ POLYURETHANE

BEFORE YOU BEGIN

One of the best ways to add new furniture pieces is to scout flea markets and tag sales. What one person no longer wants can become a "treasure" to the person who finds it.

Preparing Old Chairs

Shopping for flea market chairs can be exciting and fun. Buy the chair in the best condition that your budget will allow. It can be difficult to find identical chairs, so mix and match chairs of similar styles. A grouping of painted chairs makes an interesting conversation piece at a dining table.

Since the chairs will be painted, buying fine quality hardwood is not as critical as it would be if they were being refinished to a natural wood finish.

To decorate an old chair that is covered with built-up layers of paint, it is best to strip it down to the natural wood with a chemical stripper. Following the manufacturer's instructions, remove the layers of old paint. Since chemical strippers tend to raise the grain of the wood, it is necessary to sand the chair for a smooth surface. Be sure to wipe the chair with a soft tack cloth to remove all sanding dust before applying the base coat.

Painting Tricks

Make two, different-sized enlargements of the star design (below) to use as a template. Trace the stars onto oaktag and cut a separate stencil for each paint color used. For interesting variations:
- Use a natural sponge to paint the legs and rungs of the chairs, picking up one of the star colors.
- Use masking tape to create checkerboards or stripes by painting the untaped areas.

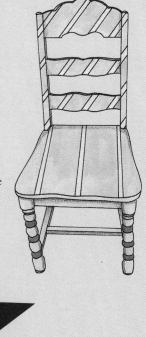

PAINTING DECORATIVE CHAIRS

HANDY HINTS

If you don't have an old chair that can be painted or can't find the style or type of chair you want at a flea market, try an unfinished furniture store for a broader selection.

1 After stripping paint from chair, repair loose joints or rungs with wood glue, making chair sturdy. Fill holes and cracks with wood putty; let dry. Sand surfaces until smooth. Wipe chair with tack cloth.

2 Apply first coat of base color to chair. Allow chair to dry completely. Using fine-grade sandpaper, remove any blemishes, then wipe clean with tack cloth. Apply second coat of paint; let dry.

3 Beginning on seat of chair, position stencil and plan design placement. Mark designs lightly with marking pencil. Place stencil on first star position and paint using stencil brush. Paint over mistakes with base coat.

OOPS

If you make a mistake while painting, it is easy to fix by just painting over or incorporating the mistake into the design.

4 Continue placing stencil and pouncing paint with stencil brush across seat and back of chair. Be sure to clean stencil brush and use new stencil for each paint color change. Add any freehand details to design at end. Seal with coat of polyurethane.

COMBED WALLS FOR TEXTURED EFFECTS

Add interest and texture to walls with a simple combing technique.

BEFORE YOU BEGIN

The illusion of a subtle or rough texture depends on the combing technique you choose to use.

Preparing the Surface

For absolutely straight lines, a smooth surface is needed for combing.
• Repair the recesses of the wall by filling dents. Repair even small scratches that may cause the comb to skip.
• To repair protrusions, sand any rough surfaces. A bump may cause the combed line to distort.
• Polish the paint for a smooth finish. Remove brush marks by wiping the base coat with a mutton cloth while the paint is still tacky.

Alternative Combing Patterns

Sweeps and swirls placed at random are the easiest designs to make.

Random U shapes provide the appearance of heavy stucco plaster (top right).

Straight lines add height if placed vertically, or width if placed horizontally. They can be used to resemble wainscoting if positioned below a chair rail and are absolutely straight.

Rigid zigzags will add an abstract, contemporary appearance to a wall.

A basket-weave design (right), with straight lines running vertically and horizontally, can produce the appearance of fabric or a checkerboard design that resembles textured tiles, depending on the width and spacing of the comb teeth.

Wavy lines, defined by uncombed areas between them, add fluidity to the wall (below, middle).

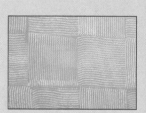

COMBING A BASKET-WEAVE PATTERN

1 After preparing a clean, smooth surface on wall (Before You Begin), use 3-inch bristle brush to apply an even base coat of paint in lighter background color. Allow paint to dry completely.

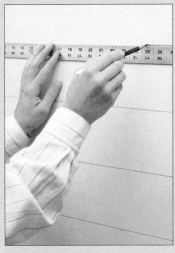

2 When paint is dry, measure width of comb. Using pencil and straightedge, lightly draw horizontal lines all the way across wall. Mark spacing for lines as far apart as width of comb.

3 Mix together equal parts of darker foreground color paint and liquid glaze. Using foam brush, apply glazed paint to a small area of the wall (the width and height of six combs). Do not allow paint to dry.

HANDY HINTS

The **typically slow** drying time of oil paint allows you to wipe away whole sections of glaze if re-combing is necessary. If latex paint is substituted for oil, add a conditioner or flow medium to the glaze to slow down the drying time.

TAKE NOTE

During the combing process, use dry rags to clean the comb often.

4 Pressing firmly, drag comb vertically through wet paint between two lines to create a combed block. Then drag comb horizontally through adjoining paint to create another combed block of the same size.

5 Continue painting and combing until whole wall is covered with checkerboard design. Clean comb often with dry rags. Allow wall to dry completely, then use bristle brush to apply one or two coats of clear polyurethane.

Verdigris-Finished Metal Furniture

Replicate the patina of verdigris with a simple paint technique.

BEFORE YOU BEGIN

Achieved naturally by exposure to the elements, a verdigris finish can be effectively imitated with paints.

Preparing the Surface

Begin by assessing the condition of the surface to be painted. It must be clean and free of dirt or rust.

Never paint over rust as it will recur and destroy the decorative finish. If the object is in relatively good condition with only small areas of rust, sand it lightly with steel wool.

To remove rust from a large area, use a wire brush or a wire wheel attached to an electric drill.

If the surface color on the object is uneven, sand it first, then apply a new base coat before using the green and white paints.

To give the object a solid base upon which to work the verdigris finish, coat it with one or two coats of latex paint in a khaki, rust, black or metallic color (below left). Use a synthetic paintbrush.

A mixture of light blue and darker green gives a delicately aged appearance (below right). If you cannot find the colors you want, you may choose to mix your own paints to obtain the exact shade you have in mind.

Authentic Touch

Make use of metallic paints for a truly authentic appearance.
• Apply copper or bronze paints over the sponged white paint to replicate the look of burnished metal where wear would naturally occur.

• Dip a dry bristle brush into the paint; brush off all the excess paint on a paper towel. Dab the brush over the sponged surface to achieve the desired effect.
• Metallic paints can also be applied after sealing, to give a shinier appearance.

PAINTING A VERDIGRIS FINISH

TAKE NOTE

Keep the second sponge clean or it will not lift off the white paint. Rinse it out frequently.

QUICK FIX

If the verdigris looks patchy after final sponging off, dab on more of the base color until the desired effect is achieved.

1 Prepare surface areas (Before You Begin). With a dabbing motion, apply green patina paint to surface. Do not cover surface evenly; small areas of base color should show through. Let base coat dry thoroughly.

2 Thin down white paint to the consistency of cream. Apply to all surfaces with a natural sponge. Because paint dries quickly, paint in small areas, no more than 6 to 10 inches.

3 Before white paint dries, use a clean, damp sponge to wipe it off. Do this unevenly, leaving extra paint in grooves and corners. Repeat application of white paint and sponging off until entire object is covered. Examine object; adjust amount of white, green or base coat until satisfied with finish.

4 When satisfied with the verdigris effect, let white paint dry completely. Spray entire surface with matte acrylic sealer, or paint on a coat of polyurethane.

LACQUERED-LOOK WOOD

Imitate the look of fine lacquered wood with paint and polyurethane.

YOU WILL NEED
- ❑ WOODEN FURNITURE
- ❑ SANDPAPER
- ❑ COTTON CLOTH
- ❑ LATEX PAINT & PRIMER
- ❑ PAINTBRUSHES
- ❑ PLASTIC DROP CLOTH
- ❑ DISPOSABLE FOAM BRUSH
- ❑ DISPOSABLE RUBBER GLOVES
- ❑ STAIN
- ❑ SPACKLING COMPOUND
- ❑ NON-YELLOWING POLYURETHANE

BEFORE YOU BEGIN

True lacquering is a difficult technique to master. But painting on several layers of latex and polyurethane is an easy way to create a comparable effect.

Knowing About Lacquer and Latex

• True lacquering uses oil-based paint and polyurethane. However, oil paints are difficult to work with, take a long time to dry and may be hard to find because of environmental regulations.
• True lacquering should last a lifetime and provide incomparable depth and quality of color.
• A lacquer effect with latex paint cannot be expected to last a lifetime. It is, however, moderately durable and offers luster and shine comparable to actual lacquering.

• For best results, use top quality brushes and paint. Poor quality bristles will leave brush marks.
• Have patience. This lacquering effect is simple, but it takes time. Each layer of paint and polyurethane must dry completely before proceeding to the next layer.
• Choose dark colors to achieve an effect with more depth.

Preparing the Surface

Remove any texture from the wood grain (top) by sanding thoroughly. The final surface of the wood should be light and smooth (bottom).

If sanding alone isn't sufficient to smooth the wood, thin down spackling compound with water. Apply with a soft cloth to cover the wood surface. Sand again.

CREATING A LACQUERED EFFECT

1 Make certain the table legs and rim are smoothly sanded. Remove any sanding residue with a cloth. Wearing rubber gloves, use a disposable foam brush to apply stain to the legs and rim of the table.

2 Sand the surface with medium grade sandpaper until it is very smooth, then paint with primer. If grain isn't smooth enough, apply spackling compound thinned with water. Sand when dry for the smoothest surface.

3 Apply three coats of latex paint, making sure each coat dries completely before applying the next. If you do not allow the paint to dry completely, the surface will be uneven and full of bubbles or cracks.

HANDY HINTS

Using a dehumidifier will help the paint dry faster. Don't attempt to use a hair dryer—you'll only succeed in creating wrinkles and cracks.

TAKE NOTE

Allow sufficient drying time for paint. When the weather is damp or humid, it takes almost three times longer for paint to dry. Wait for a dry day to paint.

4 Sand the top layer of paint and remove sanding residue with cloth. Then apply non-yellowing polyurethane. Let dry thoroughly. Apply three to four coats, sanding between each layer. After last coat, sand lightly with very fine sandpaper.

CHAMBRAY-PAINTED WALLS

Give walls new life with the subtle pattern of a chambray finish.

BEFORE YOU BEGIN

Decorate walls with a simple paint technique that actually removes paint to create the illusion of woven, textured walls. This is an easy finish for any skill level.

Preparing to Paint

For the most professional-looking job, it is essential to start with a clean, well-prepped surface. Small nicks or plaster patches will distort the finished effect.

Go over the entire wall surface, patching and sanding to smooth.

Apply painter's masking tape along the ceiling and molding and over the outlet openings. Press the tape in place with a spoon to secure and prevent paint seepage.

If possible, practice the paint technique on a small board.

Paint the prepped walls with one or two coats of the base paint.

Then apply the latex glaze over the coats of base paint. Work in small sections when applying the glaze, because it dries very quickly, often in less than 15 minutes.

It is helpful and faster to work with a partner. While one person applies the glaze, the other can go over the glaze with the dry brush, creating the woven effect.

Using Glaze

Glaze is available as an additive, making it easy to custom mix, or as a premixed paint glaze.
• The glaze must be dark enough to show over the base coat, yet transparent enough for a visible base coat.
• Generally, a latex glaze is made by mixing two parts glaze with one part paint, although color intensity should be checked on a painted surface.

PAINTING CHAMBRAY WALLS

1 Once the wall is adequately prepped and primed (Before You Begin), paint around the perimeters and corners with a finishing brush. Roll on one or two coats of base paint; let dry between coats.

2 Prepare the latex glaze (Before You Begin). Working in small sections, horizontally roll the glaze on the wall, one roller width at a time. Prevent spattering by applying the paint and glaze in thin coats.

3 With a dry brush, go over the glaze with horizontal strokes. Keep the lines as straight as possible, leaving visible brush marks. Remove excess latex glaze with a paper towel after each stroke. Keep the brush dry.

4 Continue applying paint and latex glaze over the entire wall. Allow the paint to dry thoroughly. Drying could take several hours. Once dry, repeat Steps 2 & 3, but this time working the roller and brush vertically to create the woven effect of chambray fabric.

Faux Tortoiseshell–Finished Furniture

The characteristic mottled brown surface lends a touch of intrigue.

You Will Need
- ❑ Table
- ❑ Sandpaper
- ❑ Cotton cloth
- ❑ Oil primer & yellow oil paint
- ❑ Three 2-inch natural bristle brushes
- ❑ Two 2-inch artist's brushes
- ❑ Polyurethane with maple stain (premixed)
- ❑ Black & burnt umber artist's oil paints

BEFORE YOU BEGIN

Tortoiseshell, popular in generations past for combs, spectacle frames and small ornaments, makes a comeback as an easy paint technique for furniture.

Polyurethane Pointers

Polyurethane comes in matte, semigloss and high gloss finishes. To protect furnishings painted with a tortoiseshell effect, choose high gloss. Regular polyurethane has a slightly amber cast. Some brands are available in a non-yellowing formula and some brands come premixed with stain in a variety of wood tones.
- To prepare your own mixture, blend plain polyurethane with oil-based stain or a small amount of universal tint colorant from a tube, keeping track of the amount added to match future batches.
- Do not shake cans of polyurethane or bubbles will form.
- Polyurethane finishes take 4 to 5 hours to dry.
- If necessary, thin with mineral spirits for smoother application.
- Brush gently to avoid getting air bubbles.
- Work in a room as free from dust as possible and with good ventilation.

Tortoiseshelling Tips

Traditional tortoiseshell paint finishes, which can greatly vary in pattern and in color, begin with a base of yellow and end with a top coat based on various shades of brown, sometimes shading towards orange or dark red, with black accents. Optional: Spatter the wet surface lightly with mineral spirits, then soften the spots with a dry brush.

Adapt the technique by experimenting with other color combinations to gain a mottled finish with an entirely different mood. Create a fantasy effect by pairing warm reds and pinks, for example, or top a rich sea green base with blues and deeper greens.

CREATING THE LOOK OF TORTOISESHELL

HANDY HINTS

Since the black paint has stronger impact than the burnt umber, use it sparingly. To achieve good color balance, make about five times as many squiggles with the burnt umber as with the black.

Maintain a light touch, and don't use much pressure while dragging the brush.

Tortoiseshelling works best on flat surfaces or gentle curves rather than ornately carved surfaces.

1 Sand table lightly and wipe with clean cloth. Prime with oil-based primer. Allow to dry thoroughly. Using a 2-inch natural bristle brush, paint entire table surface with a base coat of yellow oil paint. Let paint dry thoroughly.

2 With a 2-inch brush and working on one flat surface at a time, brush polyurethane stain onto the table. Tortoiseshelling requires a wet surface; continue before the polyurethane stain has had a chance to dry.

3 While the surface is still wet, lightly drag the same brush over the surface at a diagonal to the initial brush strokes. Wiggle the brush back and forth slightly to create a bit of puddling in the polyurethane stain.

OOPS

If tiny bubbles mar the finish, sand lightly after the surface has dried.

4 With the artist's brush and burnt umber oil paint, make intermittent fine squiggles about 3 to 4 inches long, beside and under the polyurethane stain squiggles. With black oil paint, make dime-sized dots and finer squiggles.

5 To blend and soften the colors, position a clean, dry 2-inch brush at table edge and gently brush over the diagonal pattern in one long stroke from left to right. Repeat from right to left.

6 Widen the pattern and make it more muted by brushing across the surface left to right at a 90° angle to the previous diagonal strokes. Reverse and go over the strokes again from right to left.

CREATIVE FLOOR DESIGN

Refurbish worn floors with decorative painting techniques.

YOU WILL NEED

- ❏ 48-INCH STRAIGHTEDGE & PENCIL
- ❏ PAINTER'S MASKING TAPE
- ❏ CRAFT KNIFE
- ❏ LATEX ACRYLIC PAINTS
- ❏ ASSORTED PAINTBRUSHES
- ❏ BLACK PERMANENT MARKER
- ❏ SMALL COIN
- ❏ POLYURETHANE
- ❏ SANDPAPER
- ❏ COTTON CLOTH

BEFORE YOU BEGIN

With their contemporary flair and old-fashioned appeal, painted floors have become one of the easiest ways to update and uplift a room.

Seeing Stars

To make a star similar to the ancient marble game, draw two overlapping triangles with 30-inch sides.

Find the center of the star shape (B). Draw a horizontal line through the center of this shape.

Then, draw a horizontal line halfway between lines A and B and another line halfway between B and C.

Begin to make the smaller triangles by making two diagonal lines through the center of the main triangle, forming an "x." Continue marking diagonal lines to fill the design with equally proportioned triangles.

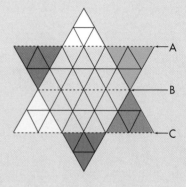

Painting Pointers

Prepare the surface of the floor for painting by removing all wax and then thoroughly cleaning.

Use fine-grade sandpaper to remove stubborn spots and stains from the floor.

If you are unsure about how the design will look on your floor, first draw it on graph paper, coloring in the designs as desired.

Designs with straight lines and simple curves will be easier to paint on the floor than intricate designs with an array of details.

Use painter's masking tape to outline the designs.

Regular masking tape will not seal as tightly, allowing paint to seep underneath.

For bright, glossy color, and a longer-lasting finish, choose semigloss paint. Flat paint has a more subdued appearance that will not withstand wear and tear if left unfinished.

Use latex paints so that spills and mistakes can be easily cleaned up with water and soap.

Polyurethane the entire floor, not just over the painted surface, so that the floor color is constant throughout the room.

PAINTING A FLOOR DESIGN

1 Find the center point of the floor; mark. Using a pencil and straightedge, draw two overlapping triangles, dividing them into smaller triangles (Before You Begin).

2 Outline the six smaller outside triangles of the star with painter's masking tape. Press the tape firmly to the floor, overlapping for better adhesion.

3 Referring to the template (Before You Begin), paint each of the six triangles with a different color acrylic paint. Let dry, then apply another coat.

4 When all the points are painted and dried, carefully remove the tape. Using a large black permanent marker, outline all the lines of the design.

5 Using a small coin and a pencil, lightly draw a circle at the intersection of each triangle. Be sure the circle is centered over the intersection. Then, use a black permanent marker to fill in each circle.

6 Allow the black-painted circles to dry completely. When dry, use a small artist's paintbrush to paint white quarter moon highlights on the circles for added effect.

7 Wipe the floor clean with a damp cloth and allow it to dry. Assess the whole design, making certain that there are no areas left unpainted. Using a wide paintbrush, apply two coats of polyurethane to the floor to protect the painted surface. Lightly sand the painted design with fine-grade sandpaper between the coats.

PAINT EFFECTS WITH PLASTIC WRAP

Give walls a pleasing two-toned effect with an easy paint technique.

YOU WILL NEED
- ❑ Latex paint & glaze
- ❑ Paint roller
- ❑ Plastic wrap
- ❑ Trash barrel

BEFORE YOU BEGIN

Ordinary plastic wrap, borrowed from the kitchen, takes on a new role as an inexpensive and effective tool for a simple paint treatment. The result: walls decorated with patterns ranging from muted and feathery to striking.

Preparing to Paint

Before painting, mask off the ceiling and the base-board with painter's masking tape to keep the adjacent areas clean.

To provide a base coat for the textured glaze, cover the walls with eggshell-finish latex paint in the desired color.

For the glaze coat, mix a second latex color with an equal amount of latex glaze.

For a subtle effect, choose top and base colors very similar in tone or value. The slightly mottled result pro-vides a good base for sten-cils or stamps.

To create a more dramatic effect for the wall, select two highly contrasting colors. Or, choose the base color and then drastically lighten or darken it for the top coat.

Experiment with a few dif-ferent ways to crinkle the plastic wrap. Blot off the latex/glaze coat with hand-fuls of scrunched plastic (top left), wrap plastic around a roller (center) or press the plastic flat onto the wall, using your hands to wrinkle it (bottom right).

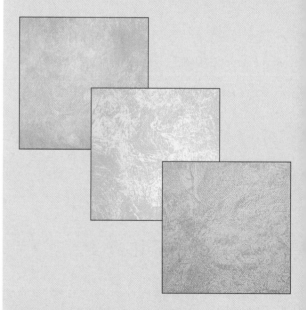

Plastic Pointers

• Equip the work area with plenty of plastic wrap and tear off a new piece as soon as the previous one is loaded with paint.
• Lightweight latex gloves can help keep hands clean, but don't use them if they prevent a good grip on the plastic wrap.
• If a defined line forms between adjoining rows or glaze, dab the overlap with crinkled plastic to make the transition appear seamless.

CREATING TEXTURE WITH PLASTIC WRAP

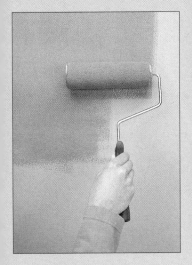

HANDY HINTS

When crinkling the plastic wrap on the wall, try to avoid using your fingertips, which can leave very definite impressions. Keep your hands as flat as possible during the process.

Don't try to unroll and cut the plastic ahead of time because it will cling to itself mercilessly. Unroll each length on the wall as needed.

1 After the base coat dries, use a paint roller slightly wider than a roll of plastic wrap to roll a vertical line of the latex/glaze mixture (Before You Begin) onto the wall. Paint from the ceiling to the floor in long, straight strokes.

2 While the latex/glaze mixture is still wet, unroll a few inches of the plastic wrap and press into the paint at the ceiling line. Continue unrolling plastic carefully down to the baseboard and trim it off.

3 Keeping your hands as flat as possible, scrunch up the plastic wrap as desired on the wall. More wrinkles in the wrap will yield a highly textured finished wall; fewer wrinkles leave a smoother look.

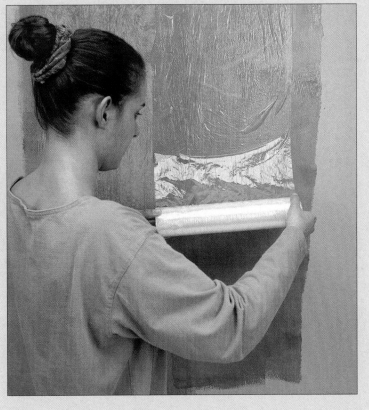

4 Starting at the ceiling line, very carefully peel the plastic wrap away from the wall. Keep a trash barrel lined with a plastic liner bag handy and immediately dispose of the paint-saturated plastic wrap.

5 Repeat Steps 1 through 4 for the remaining wall, overlapping the previous row slightly. If a line or "seam" forms, apply more latex/glaze to the area and re-wrinkle with plastic wrap, keeping the edges up. Alternatively, dab overlap with crinkled plastic to blend seam.

PAINTED STONE EFFECTS FOR FLOORS

Painted squares in tones of gray evoke the stylish look of slate.

YOU WILL NEED

- ❑ PRIMER & ROLLER
- ❑ SEMIGLOSS LATEX PAINT
- ❑ TAPE MEASURE & PENCIL
- ❑ ¼-INCH-WIDE MASKING TAPE
- ❑ 2-INCH-WIDE LOW-TACK PAPER MASKING TAPE
- ❑ GLAZING LIQUID
- ❑ 3-INCH FOAM BRUSHES & ARTIST'S PAINTBRUSH
- ❑ RUBBER GLOVES
- ❑ PLASTIC BAGS
- ❑ POLYURETHANE
- ❑ SANDPAPER

BEFORE YOU BEGIN

Create a deceptively realistic stone effect on any smooth-surfaced floor with three shades of gray latex paint and these simple steps.

Preparation

Using sharp scissors, cut a lightweight plastic drop sheet or dry cleaner's bag into rectangles that are 6 inches wider and three times longer than the size of the tile square.

Using a paintbrush or roller, paint the floor with primer and let it dry thoroughly. Then apply two coats of semigloss latex in the color desired for the "grout" between the painted tiles.

Designing on the Diagonal

A diagonal design produces a sense of motion, creating an optical illusion that makes the floor appear larger than it actually is.
• To plot a diagonal pattern in a perfectly square room, snap a chalk line diagonally from corner to corner to form an X and mark the center of the room. Working from the center out, use a T square to measure and mark the squares; mark off the diagonal grid with masking tape.

• To plot a diagonal pattern in a rectangular room, decide on the size of the "stones" and cut a paper template to this size. Fold the template in half diagonally. Starting at the center point of the most noticeable wall, put the folded edge of the template against the baseboard and use the template as a guide to mark the whole squares between. Plot the grid on the rest of floor; mask off the grid with tape.

PAINTING A FAKE STONE FLOOR

1 Prime floor and apply "grout color" paint as base (Before You Begin). Using a tape measure and pencil, make dots on floor at 18-inch intervals along room edges. Begin at most visible point of room so that any partial squares will be least conspicuous.

2 Draw intersecting lines to form a grid with 18-inch squares covering entire floor. Run strips of ¼-inch masking tape across length and width of room to mask off "grout" lines of grid.

3 To make sure painted squares will have "clean" edges, mask off every other square with 2-inch-wide, low-tack paper masking tape. (Low-tack paper masking tape is sticky along one edge only.)

HANDY HINTS

Keep reusing the same plastic until it no longer picks up paint and glaze. Rearrange the bunched up plastic as you proceed, to vary the imprint on the floor and imitate the natural texture of stone.

Plot the design so that any partial blocks fall evenly around the perimeter of the room or are hidden in an inconspicuous spot (beneath a piece of furniture, for example).

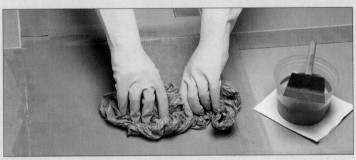

4 Mix one part medium gray semigloss with four parts water-based glazing liquid. Apply to first square with a 3-inch foam brush; brush toward center to keep edges neat.

5 Bunch up one piece of plastic. Roll plastic over and over across glaze on entire square; be careful that paint does not extend onto adjoining squares. Plastic will pick up some of paint/glaze mix and leave a stone-like pattern behind it. Repeat with remaining unmasked squares and let dry. Remove tape and mask off edges of painted squares.

6 Repeat Steps 4 and 5 with darkest gray semigloss. Remove tape as soon as possible, pulling it up gently as each row of "tiles" is completed.

7 Touch up major runs with a small artist's brush. Touch up inside squares with plastic bags or foam brushes, masking off adjoining squares, if necessary. Let dry thoroughly. Apply two coats of water-based polyurethane for floors, allowing each coat to dry thoroughly. Sand lightly before the next application.

DECORATING
PROJECTS

Focus your creativity on the details of your home—both inside and out. Re-cover a removable seat on an accent chair. Add a tasteful sheer curtain to a difficult arched window. Update your entertainment center with some simple trim molding. Brighten your lawn chairs with fresh covers. Create a simple awning for your patio. These projects will help you solve the decorating challenges you have always wanted to tackle.

RE-COVERED REMOVABLE SEAT

Alter the mood of a room by applying new fabric to chair seats.

YOU WILL NEED

❏ FABRIC
❏ STAPLE GUN & ⅜- OR
   5/16-INCH STAPLES
❏ PLIERS
❏ FABRIC SHEARS

BEFORE YOU BEGIN

Re-covering a removable seat doesn't require upholstering or sewing skills, and it easily dresses up the whole room.

Selecting the Covering

• Use a tightly woven, sturdy cotton or wool fabric for the cushion cover so it will withstand heavy use.

• Spray on a protective treatment for further insurance against spills on dining chair cushions.

Removing the Seat and Fabric

Some seat cushions pop out when pushed up; others are screwed in place at the corners (below top). Save screws for reassembly after changing the fabric cover. If screw holes have enlarged over time, wedge a sliver of wood into the opening before tightening the screw securely.

Use pliers to remove tacks or staples that hold the fabric in place (below bottom). Work carefully so that the fabric remains intact. Use the original fabric cover as the basis for cutting out new fabric for the seat.

Check the cushion for wear. If it is out of shape or shredding, replace the foam.

Use a muslin fabric to cover the underside of the cushion to conceal the raw edges and staples. Or use an inexpensive cotton that matches the color of the top fabric. Cut the muslin to the same size as the cushion base. Place fabric right side up on base of cushion to finish the underside of the seat.

RE-COVERING THE CUSHION

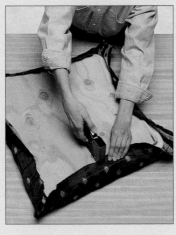

1 Lay fabric right side down. Cut out a fabric cover that is 3 inches wider on all sides than original cover. Place cushion and base over fabric. Check the right side to make sure the design is properly centered.

2 Pull fabric edges over to bottom of cushion base. Using a staple gun, staple center of each side in place, holding fabric taut. Again, check right side of cushion to make sure pattern is properly aligned.

3 Holding fabric taut, staple it around base. Keep staples ½ inch from edge and 1 inch apart. Work from center of each side of cushion out toward corners. Staple one side and its opposite, then the remaining sides.

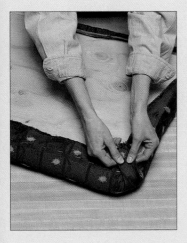

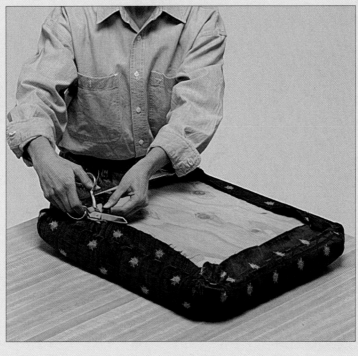

4 At the corners, make tiny folds and tucks to ease the fabric around the corner, making sure it doesn't look pleated. Before stapling, check the right side to make certain the edge is smooth. Staple in place.

5 Trim excess fabric to within 1 inch of the staples. If you plan to cover the underside of the cushion, cut muslin to fit and press ½ inch under all sides. Staple cover in place, keeping staples 2 to 3 inches apart. Then slip the seat cushion back onto the chair and replace the screws.

ENTERTAINMENT CENTER MAKEOVER

Turn old shelves into a one-of-a kind unit with molding and paint.

YOU WILL NEED

- ❏ ENTERTAINMENT CENTER
- ❏ DECORATIVE MOLDING
- ❏ MITER BOX & SAW
- ❏ WOOD GLUE, HAMMER & No.4 FINISHING NAILS
- ❏ ¾-INCH HEADLESS BRADS
- ❏ TARP
- ❏ PAINTBRUSH & ROLLER
- ❏ 2-INCH PAINTBRUSH
- ❏ PRECUT ¼-INCH-THICK MIRRORS & ADHESIVE
- ❏ ⅜-INCH-THICK GLASS SHELVES
- ❏ LIGHTING UNITS
- ❏ NEW HARDWARE (OPTIONAL)

BEFORE YOU BEGIN

Some paint and a few designer touches can easily help turn a cheap entertainment center into a modern display unit.

Preparation

- Measure the old unit (illustrated below) to determine the mirror and molding sizes. If the mirrors need to be a non-standard size, have them cut at a glass shop.
- If new handles don't fit, fill the old holes with putty and drill new ones.
- Sand the entire unit with No. 80 sandpaper; wipe clean. Prime the surface with white paint.
- Measure the depth and width of the unit. Use the 45-degree slot of a miter box to cut the dentil and crown molding to the right length.

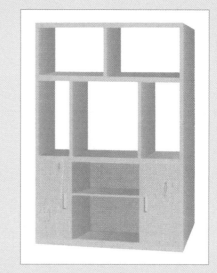

DECORATING THE ENTERTAINMENT CENTER

1 Starting with the front of unit, use wood glue to attach dentil molding along top edge. Secure molding with No. 4 nails. Attach sides, making sure mitered corners fit snugly.

2 Nail crown molding in place along top of dentil molding, starting with front piece and finishing with side pieces. Make sure there is no gap between dentil and crown moldings.

3 Remove doors. Draw a rectangle in the center of each door, 2 inches from edges. Cut ¾-inch panel molding to fit markings; miter at 45-degree angle. Use brads to secure along lines. Paint doors.

6 Apply mirror adhesive every 3 to 4 inches on back of mirrors. Position mirrors on back wall of unit between upper and lower shelves. Adhesive dries quickly, so make sure mirrors are placed correctly the first time.

4 Protect surrounding area with tarps or newspaper. Paint molding and unit edges with main color paint; let dry. If desired, splatter with contrast paints; splatter darker color paint first.

5 Paint remainder of unit with main color. Use a 2-inch brush for cutting in corners. Allow to dry; apply a second coat. Make sure paint covers any unwanted splattering on main body of unit.

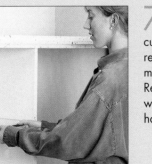

7 For unobstructed lighting, replace shelves with glass cut to fit. Slide them onto pegs remaining from original shelves, making sure pegs are secure. Reattach doors for lower shelves with new hardware (hinges and handles).

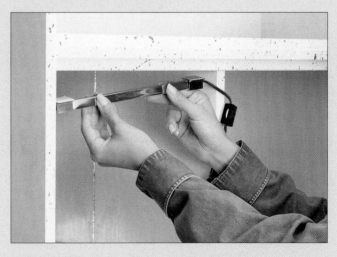

8 Measure and mark placement of lighting units. Install behind molding above mirrored area, according to manufacturer's instructions. Run cords through holes in back of unit to keep them out of sight.

Re-Covered Lawn Chairs

Rejuvenate lawn chairs with bright new fabrics for summer.

BEFORE YOU BEGIN

Don't discard sturdy-framed lawn chairs just because the seat is worn. Replacing the frayed webbing with stylish fabric makes it better than new.

Removing the Old Webbing

Prior to creating a new seat cover, remove the existing worn webbing. The webbing is usually screwed or clipped in place at the bottom, top and side rails. Cutting off the webbing with sharp scissors or a utility knife releases the tension on the screws or clips and facilitates removal.

Save the screws or clips in a container or self-sealing plastic bag so they will not get lost in the shuffle; the new chair cover will require the fasteners along the top and the bottom.

Planning Fabric and Grommets

Replacing a seat cover requires two fabric rectangles that are identical.

To determine the width of the rectangle, measure the width of the seat from side rail to side rail (a).

To determine the length of the material, measure from the top rail, down behind the center back rail, to the front rail (b), then add 5 to 6 inches for folding over the top rail and front rail, depending on their widths.

For the grommets, measure from the top rail to the center of the chair and calculate how many grommets can fit about every 2 inches; repeat for the seat (c). Double this amount to have enough for both side edges.

SEWING A LAWN CHAIR COVER

1 Press under 2 inches on the long sides of both fabric pieces. Pin the two pieces together with the wrong sides facing, matching the folds and the raw edges. Topstitch 1¼ inch in from the folded edges and then ¼ inch in.

2 Mark placement for the grommets every 2 inches along the folded edges, equidistant between the fold and the stitching line. To determine placement for the top grommet, test scrap fabric on the chair.

3 Insert the grommets, per manufacturer's instructions, along the sides of the fabric. Pull the fabric over the top rail and attach it with the clips or screws, folding under the raw edges to prevent fraying.

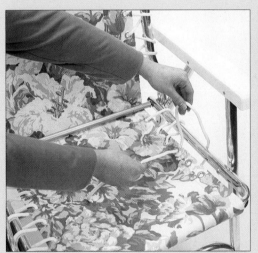

4 Pull the fabric under the center rail and then over the bottom rail of the chair. Keep the fabric taut to ensure firm support for seating. Fasten the fabric firmly under the chair's front rail with the clips.

5 Working from back to front, thread the rope through the top grommets on each side. Pull the rope until the two lengths are equal. Then, working on both sides at one time, wind the rope around the chair rails and into each succeeding grommet until the entire chair is laced. Be sure the rope tensions stay the same and the distances from the rails to the grommets are equal.

6 Pull the rope taut to prevent sagging. Tie the rope ends securely into a knot underneath the front of the chair. Trim the rope ends, but be sure to leave enough to discourage fraying and permit reknotting if necessary.

No-Sew Privacy Shade

Make unique shades that pull up from the bottom of the window.

BEFORE YOU BEGIN

Shades that operate from the bottom up are an original way to let light in while keeping a room private. Understanding the mechanics is key.

Selecting Fabrics

Closely woven, stable fabrics are best to use. Strong linen, cotton and cotton/polyester blends are suitable. Avoid sheer and loosely woven fabrics.

• Prints, whether large or small scale, accent a window and introduce a strong design element. Plain colors are more functional and blend into the decor.

• The addition of a heavy-weight fusible craft backing or stabilizer is essential for maintaining crisp pleats or smooth roller shades. Always test it first on a fabric scrap to determine fabric compatibility and the final look.

• Use drapery-weight nylon cording for strength and durability.

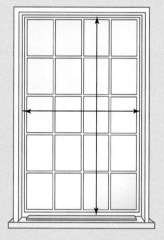

Calculating Materials

Measure the height and width of the window, from inside frame edge to inside frame edge.

The finished size of the shade should be 1½ times the window height measurement and ½ inch narrower than the width measurement. Use these figures to determine fabric yardage and cut sizes for the stabilizer and fabric.

For a mounting board, cut a ¼-inch by 2-inch wood strip ⅛ inch to ¼ inch shorter than the finished width of the shade.

Cut one nylon cord equal to four times the height of the window, plus two times the width, plus an extra 12 inches for the right side of the shade. Cut a second cord equal to four times the window height, plus 12 inches for the left side.

MAKING THE SHADE

1 Cut the stabilizer the exact size of the finished shade (Before You Begin). Cut the fabric 2 inches longer and wider than stabilizer to allow for four hems. Center the stabilizer on wrong side of fabric.

2 Press 1 inch top, bottom and side hems to the wrong side of the shade, beginning with side hems. Place a strip of double-sided fusible web under the hem, fold down and fuse hem in place.

3 Using an air-soluble marker and a straightedge on the wrong side of the shade, begin at the shade's bottom edge and mark horizontal foldlines 3 inches apart across the width of the shade.

4 Crease the fabric along the marked foldlines and press each 3-inch pleat in place, making sure the pleat edges are sharp and straight. Accordion fold the pleats as they are completed.

5 With an awl, punch holes in the center of the fabric pleats, 3 inches in from each side edge. On each side, feed a cord through the holes from bottom to top, leaving the cord ends unattached.

6 Attach screw eyes 3 inches from the ends of the mounting board. Tie the cord bottom ends to the screw eyes. Attach the mounting board and bottom pleat to the windowsill with screws.

7 Mount two screw eyes to the upper window frame, aligning them with screw eyes on the mounting board. Mount a cleat on the left window frame.

8 Feed the right cord through the upper right screw eye, across the window, through the upper left screw eye and down to the cleat mounted next to the window. Then wrap the cord around the cleat, bring the cord back up through both screw eyes and down to the shade's right edge. Knot the cord end through the shade's top hole. Feed the left cords through the upper left screw eye and down to the cleat. Repeat the wrapping and knotting process described above.

Decorative Patio Awning

A festive awning creates unique decor on your patio.

YOU WILL NEED

- ❑ STRIPED CANVAS
- ❑ SCISSORS & PINS
- ❑ SEWING MACHINE
- ❑ IRON & IRONING BOARD
- ❑ 1X3 BOARD
- ❑ GROMMET KIT
- ❑ METAL OR PVC PIPING & CORNER PIECES
- ❑ HOOK BOLT & DRILL

BEFORE YOU BEGIN

Stitch up this fresh-looking awning and you'll have a simple tent roof to block the run's rays. Open sides will let summer breezes waft through.

Cutting the Canvas

To create an awning that measures approximately 8 by 10 feet, purchase 22 yards of striped canvas that measures at least 48 inches in width.

Cut the fabric into two 11-foot lengths. Allow extra fabric for matching stripes or making dimensions larger.

Choose materials that are sturdy enough to withstand the elements.

Attaching the Awning

• Decide on placement for fastening the awning to the house. The greater the difference between the height of the hooks on the house and the height of the support poles in front, the more pronounced the awning's roof-like angle.

• The drape of the fabric depends on the distance between the support poles and the house. Placing the poles slightly closer gives the fabric a gentle swag. For a more tailored look, minimize the drape of the material by placing poles farther from the house.

Means of Support

• Mark the hook placement to hold the awning at its outer edges and in the middle. Double check the markings with a level to make sure the awning will hang straight.

• Drill pilot holes and screw in three zinc-plated or galvanized hook bolts. Found in hardware stores, zinc-plated hook bolts will not rust when used outdoors, nor will they stain house or fabric.

MAKING THE AWNING

1 Join two widths of fabric with right sides together, carefully matching stripes to create basic awning shape. Press seam open. If desired, stitch as close as possible to edge of seam so it will remain flat and not fray.

2 To finish outer edges of awning material, fold, press and stitch a ½-inch hem if woven selvage is intact. If not, press edge under ½ inch; then press ½ inch again. Stitch along inner fold through all layers.

3 At front edge of canvas, press under ½ inch; then press under 4 inches. Pin and stitch along inner fold to form a pocket for awning support poles. Press again once the stitching is completed.

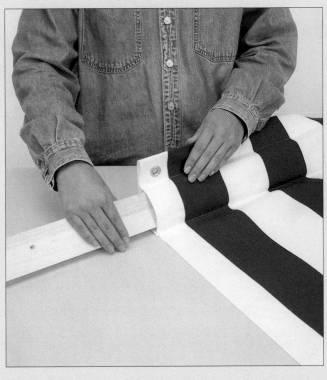

4 At back edge of canvas, press under ½ inch; then press under 6 inches. Stitch along inner fold. Measure, mark and sew a line of stitching 2 inches from top of canvas to make a pocket for 1x3 and a heading for grommets.

5 Fold fabric in half widthwise to determine center. Mark placements for three grommets, each 1 inch down from top edge of awning; one at either side; third in center. Make sure marks match hook placement on wall.

6 Install grommets according to package instructions. Slide 1x3 into pocket below grommets. Slide piping into front pocket of awning. Assemble piping with corner pieces. Loop grommets over hook bolts on wall. Fix pipe supports into ground.

Updated Deck or Director's Chair

Revitalize outdoor chairs with simple-to-sew, vibrant fabric covers.

YOU WILL NEED

❑ DECK CHAIR OR
   DIRECTOR'S CHAIR
❑ MEASURING TAPE
❑ HEAVYWEIGHT FABRIC
❑ SEWING MACHINE
❑ IRON & IRONING BOARD
❑ PINS & THREAD

BEFORE YOU BEGIN

Use old chair covers as patterns for new covers and to determine yardage.

Measurements

• Carefully cut the old chair cover off the frame. Lay it over the new fabric as a pattern for the new cover.

• For the director's chair, add ½-inch seam allowances at top and bottom and 2 inches on sides. For the deck chair, add 3-inch seam allowances at top and bottom and ½ inch on both sides.

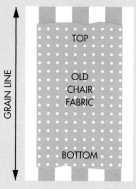

DECK CHAIR

GRAIN LINE

TOP

OLD CHAIR FABRIC

BOTTOM

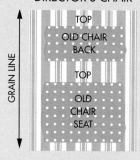

DIRECTOR'S CHAIR

GRAIN LINE

TOP
OLD CHAIR BACK

TOP
OLD CHAIR SEAT

MAKING A DIRECTOR'S CHAIR COVER

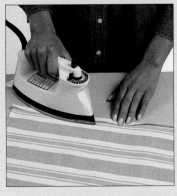

1 Make double hems at the top and bottom edges of the back and seat pieces. To double hem, press under ¼ inch to wrong side of each long edge, then press under ¼ inch again. Stitch close to folded edge.

2 To create the rod pockets that fit the chair back and seat pieces onto the frame, press the fabric ½ inch to the wrong side of each short edge of the chair back. Repeat at each short edge of the seat piece.

3 Press each short edge under another 2½ inches toward wrong side. Stitch close to folded edge. Stitch again ¼ inch from previous stitching to reinforce. This will create rod pockets at each end.

TAKE NOTE

If the old chair cover is worn, it may also have become stretched out of shape. In this case, measure the distance from dowel edge to dowel edge for an accurate measure of the finished seat width. Add rod pocket and hem inches to width measurement as noted in Before You Begin.

MAKING A DECK CHAIR COVER

4 Press seat and back pieces. Insert dowels or chair slats into pocket openings and slip the new covers onto the old chair frame. Apply a water- and stain-repellent finish to protect regular fabrics.

1 Most deck chairs are a standard size, so it is possible to buy packages of pre-measured lengths of deck chair fabric. In this case, the side edges do not require seaming. If the old cover is not available, wrap a tape measure around the top bar and drape it into a comfortable-looking curve. Then wrap the tape measure over the bottom bar to determine yardage. Cut fabric to the right size. Press under ¼ inch and then ¼ inch again along long edges. Stitch close to folds.

2 To create a pocket opening for the dowels, press ½ inch to wrong side of top and bottom edges. Press under again, this time 2½ inches. Stitch close to folded edge. Stitch again ¼ inch from previous stitching to reinforce.

3 Press seat cover. Insert dowels in pocket openings to hang new cover on chair. Attach dowels to chair. If chair itself is looking old and worn, paint the frame before hanging the new cover.

SHEER TREATMENTS FOR ARCHED WINDOWS

Sheer fabric emphasizes the beauty of an arched window.

YOU WILL NEED

❏ ADJUSTABLE CURVED
   ROD
❏ 2 TENSION RODS FOR
   LOWER WINDOW
❏ MEASURING TAPE
❏ SCISSORS
❏ LACE FABRIC
❏ RUBBER BAND
❏ BUTTONHOLE TWIST
   THREAD
❏ CHALK

BEFORE YOU BEGIN

A lacy fan and shirred panel provide privacy in an arched window.

Measuring

For top, place curved rod in arch and adjust it to fit.
• To determine fabric cut width, measure from top of arch down to bottom of rosette position. Add 1½ times rod diameter for rod pocket; 6 inches for header; ½ inch for hem; and 3½ inches for rosette.
• For fabric length, lay curved rod out flat and measure distance from end to end. Add 2½ to 3 times this measurement for finished cut length.

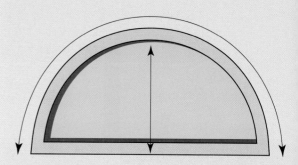

Next, determine bottom panel fabric measurements.
• To determine bottom panel cut length, measure from top tension rod to lower rod position. Add 3 times diameter of rod for rod pockets and 3 inches for 1½-inch bottom ruffle.
• To determine cut width, multiply rod length (or window width) by 2½ or 3, depending on desired fullness.

MAKING AN ARCHED WINDOW TREATMENT

HANDY HINTS

Found at fabric or home decorating stores, adjustable curved rods are the perfect solution for arched windows. Mounted inside the arch frame, the rods fit snugly inside the window casing, placing the curtains close to the glass. Adjust the curved rod to fit the arch before hanging the window treatment.

1 On arch piece, turn under ¼ inch on one long side. Stitch in place. Along finished long edge, fold down 3 inches plus 1½ times rod diameter to wrong side. Stitch close to edge. Stitch 3 inches from fold for header and rod pocket.

2 Turn under and press ¼ inch along remaining three sides and stitch in place. Eliminate bulk on very fine or extremely sheer fabrics by zigzag- or serge-finishing raw edges, rather than turning under hem.

3 Insert curved rod into pocket and position in arch. Hand-gather lower edge hem to center and secure with rubber band. Pull and spread fabric out from rubber band to make rosette and secure with button-hole twist thread.

6 With right side of fabric down, turn up bottom edge ¼ inch and press. Then, stitch in place. Mark up from finished edge 3 inches plus 1½ times rod diameter. Fold finished edge to mark and pin. Stitch close to edge to secure.

4 Cut fabric according to measurements for lower shirred panel. Turn under and press ¼ inch, then ¼ inch again along each long side for hems. With matching thread, stitch side hems close to edge.

5 With right side of fabric down, fold and press down ¼ inch along top edge; stitch. From finished edge, measure down 1½ times rod diameter; mark. Fold finished edge to marks and stitch to create top rod pocket.

7 Measure up 1½ inches from folded edge and mark. Pin layers together when working with fine or lace fabrics to prevent fabric from shifting while stitching. Stitch along marks creating rod pocket and ruffle at lower edge of panel. Place panel on two tension rods at top and bottom and hang inside window molding.

Whimsical Window Cornice

Add handcrafted charm to any room with painted-wood cornices.

You Will Need

- ☐ ¼-INCH PLYWOOD
- ☐ CARBON PAPER & PENCIL
- ☐ HANDSAW
- ☐ SANDPAPER
- ☐ PAINT & PRIMER
- ☐ 1- & 2-INCH BRUSHES
- ☐ ¹⁄₆₄-INCH ALUMINUM SHEET
- ☐ METAL SHEARS
- ☐ STAPLE GUN & ¼-INCH STAPLES
- ☐ GREASE PENCIL
- ☐ AWL & HAMMER
- ☐ 3 FEET OF ¼-INCH ARMATURE WIRE
- ☐ FINISHING NAILS
- ☐ ANGLE IRONS

BEFORE YOU BEGIN

Original and full of fun, cornice window treatments are surprisingly easy to make and mount.

Measuring and Mounting

If installing blinds, shades or curtains, measure for cornice and mounting board after treatments are secured.

- For cornice width, find distance between outside edges of window frame, plus 2 to 3 inches on each end for rods or blind hardware.
- For mounting board depth, measure from rod or blind clearance to wall, plus 3 inches.
- For mounting board width, subtract 5 inches from finished width of cornice.

- For securing mounting board on back of cornice, mark a placement line 1 inch below the center of cornice.

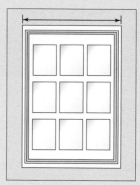

Using the Template

Enlarge template (below) on photocopier or graph paper by about 765%.

Trace house design onto plywood with carbon paper and pencil, using separate template for each house.

Vary widths of houses, windows and roof styles as desired for interest. Five houses will fit across a 49½-inch-wide window (from frame edge to frame edge).

Use handsaw to cut out house shapes along markings. Cut separate templates for each roof. Sand rough edges before painting.

MAKING THE CORNICE

1 Transfer template to plywood (Before You Begin). Use a handsaw to cut outer edges of template shape. Sand rough edges. Using a 2-inch brush, paint both sides of the mounting board and cornice with one coat of primer; let dry completely.

2 Paint each house front in different colors; let dry. Using the template (Before You Begin) and a pencil, outline windows and doors. With a 1-inch foam brush, paint the designs. Allow to dry thoroughly.

3 Using metal shears, cut roofs from aluminum sheeting; add 1½ inch for upper edge overlap. Align metal on rooftops. Fold overlaps to the back; staple them in place with a staple gun.

HANDY HINTS

Most lumberyards will cut boards and lumber into simple shapes for a small fee. Or, use a coping saw or jigsaw, if you have one, to cut out the house shapes.

In place of an awl, use a hammer and nail to create the decorative designs and patterns on the house rooftops.

TAKE NOTE

Beware of sharp metal edges when working with sheet aluminum. Wear heavy work gloves to protect your hands.

4 Create decorative designs on the roofs with a grease pencil. Then, using an awl and hammer, punch the designs. For chimney smoke, bend armature wire into curls and staple them to back of chimney.

5 With 1-inch finishing nails, attach primed mounting board to cornice. Measure and then screw two 3-inch angle irons to the top of the window frame, one at each end. Screw the mounting board to the angle irons, centering the painted cornice over the window.

No-Sew Appliqué Pillow

Easy, appliquéd pillows will add pizzazz to any special occasion.

YOU WILL NEED

❏ 14-INCH PILLOW FORM
❏ VARIETY OF FABRIC
  PIECES
❏ TAILOR'S CHALK
❏ 1 YARD PAPER-BACKED
  FUSIBLE WEB
❏ FABRIC PAINTS
❏ MARKING PEN
❏ SEWING MACHINE
❏ THREAD & SCISSORS
❏ IRON & IRONING BOARD

BEFORE YOU BEGIN

Appliqué the easy way by fusing fabric shapes to a base cloth then finishing the edges with paint.

Preparing the Pillow and Pattern Pieces

• You will need nine 5- by 5-inch squares of fabric to cut out the fruit shapes, ¼ yard fabric to cut the cornucopia and one 12-inch square of fabric to cut out its mouth.
• Use tailor's chalk to mark a 14-inch square in the center of the pillow front.
• For the pillow front, cut a 15-inch square piece of fabric.

• For the pillow back, cut two 8- by 15-inch rectangles.
• For the rectangle under the cornucopia base, cut a 7- by 14-inch rectangle.
• Use a photocopier to enlarge the pattern pieces to size. Trace the shapes and transfer the tracings to the back of fusible webbing. Cut out each shape and iron it onto the desired fabric.

Paint Pointers

Fabric paints are ideal for adding colorful style to appliquéd pillows.
• Hold the tip of the paint bottle close to the fabric and squeeze out the paint with gentle, even pressure.

• Let the design dry flat for at least 24 hours before using the pillow.
• Let the paint dry for at least 72 hours before washing the pillow. Do not tumble dry.

APPLIQUÉING WITHOUT SEWING

HANDY HINTS

When fusing the appliqués to the background, do not move the iron back and forth. Instead, place the iron directly over the appliqué and leave it in place for a few seconds.

DOLLAR SENSE

Use scraps of fabrics left over from other projects. Try to combine pieces that will someday be of sentimental value. Scraps from children's back-to-school clothes, pieces from your first handmade curtains, or quilt project leftovers can all become treasures.

1 Cut fabric pieces and apply fusible web (Before You Begin). Remove paper backing from rectangular appliqué; iron onto bottom of front piece. Fuse cornucopia shape, fruits and leaves in place, starting with cornucopia. Overlap pieces as necessary.

2 Finish all fabric edges with fabric paint. Squeeze-tube fabric paints are easiest to control. Use enough paint to cover all raw edges. Add stems and highlight leaves with paint. Allow to dry completely according to manufacturer's instructions.

3 To finish pillow, turn under ½ inch along one long edge of each back piece; topstitch. With right sides together, pin back pieces to front piece, overlapping topstitched edges in center of back to form opening.

4 With right sides together, sew pillow front to pillow back pieces with a ½-inch seam allowance. Trim seams and clip corners; turn pillow cover right side out. Insert pillow form through opening in back.

WOOD

CRAFTS

Using a few simple tools and materials, you can build amazing creations from wood! You don't even have to be a woodworking pro. You'll find simple shelves, storage and display solutions, picture frames and other great projects here—all complete with step-by-step instructions that take away any how-to guesswork. Then finish your creation with paint or stain to match your decor, and add designs or hardware that celebrate your own personal style.

DECORATIVE MODULAR STORAGE BOXES

Eliminate clutter with a display of modular storage cubes.

BEFORE YOU BEGIN

A modular system is made by hanging same-size boxes together. To add more storage space, make slotted inserts to create shelves within the boxes.

Each cube of the modular storage system shown at left measures 8 inches deep by 13 inches. To make one cube, you will need to obtain the following pieces of wood:

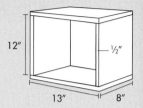

From clear pine or poplar: two pieces ½ by 8 by 13 inches and four pieces ½ by 8 by 12 inches.

From birch plywood: one piece ¼ by 13 by 13 inches.

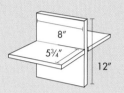

Decorating Ideas

There are many ways to use paint, paper and other materials to decorate a modular storage box, turning it into a focal point.
• Use wallpaper to cover the inside and/or outside.
• Stencil around outsides.

• Add mirrors to the sides or inside back wall of each cube.
• Paint the front edges of the box a different color than the body.
• Paint each of the cubes a different color.

Compartment Planning

To help you plan the size of the compartments in your modular storage box, here are standard sizes of items you might want to store. Be sure to allow at least ¼ inch all around for easy access.
• Paperback book: 6⅞ by 4¼ inches.
• Standard book: 9½ by 7 inches.

• Large book: 11 by 9 inches.
• Art book: 15 by 11 inches.
• Record album: 12⅜ by 12⅜ inches.
• Videotape: 7½ by 4⅛ inches.
• DVD: 7⅛ by 5⅜ inches.
• Compact disc: 5 by 5½ inches.
• Audio tape: 4¼ by 2¾ inches.

BUILDING A MODULAR UNIT

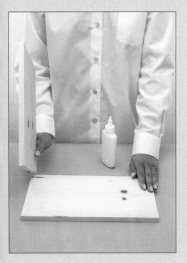

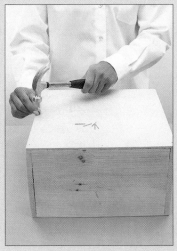

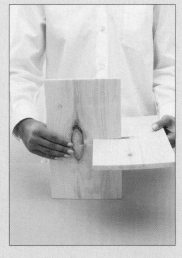

1 Assemble a square box by gluing two 12-inch pieces of pine onto opposite ends of one 13-inch piece. Secure with 1-inch brads. Glue second 13-inch piece on top of 12-inch pieces to form a square. Secure with brads.

2 Position 13-inch plywood square on four edges of box to form backing. Glue and secure with brads. Check that all pieces fit evenly, with no gaps. Hammer in additional brads as needed.

3 Mark a line across middle of depth of two remaining 12-inch pieces. Cut a ½-inch wide by 4-inch deep slot centered along each line (Before You Begin). Position cut slots into each other to form insert. Slide insert into box.

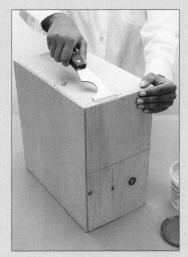

4 Use a ruler and pencil to draw a line on each side of box, indicating center of insert boards. Hammer brads along lines to secure inserts inside box. Erase pencil marks if box will be finished with clear stain.

5 Use wood putty to fill any gaps in seams and to cover brads. Allow putty to dry according to manufacturer's instructions. Sand entire box, particularly areas with putty, to prepare for painting. Apply primer to seal wood and provide a base coat for paint.

6 Allow primer to dry completely. Paint box desired color, working from top to bottom. For an interesting, two-tone effect, use a different color paint inside box.

CUSTOMIZED SPICE RACK

Create specialty storage space with decorative spice racks.

YOU WILL NEED

- ❑ ½ BY 2½-INCH PINE BOARDS
- ❑ ½ BY 3¼-INCH PINE BOARDS
- ❑ ¾ BY 9½-INCH PINE BOARDS
- ❑ HAMMER & NAILS
- ❑ WOOD GLUE & FILLER
- ❑ ARTIST'S TRANSFER PAPER
- ❑ TAPE MEASURE
- ❑ PAINTBRUSH & PAINTS
- ❑ CLEAR-DRYING VARNISH
- ❑ BRACKETS

BEFORE YOU BEGIN

Planks of 1x3 pine are easy to work with because the sides and edges are smooth and the surface has few knotholes. Use a handsaw to cut the boards.

Prep Work

Cut and sand the pieces listed for each size of wood.

From ½ by 2½-inch pine:
A: three pieces 3 inches long
B: one piece 6 inches long
C: two pieces 9½ inches long
D: one piece 12 inches long
E: one piece 8½ inches long.

From ½ by 3¼-inch pine:
F: two pieces 13 inches long

From ¾ by 9½-inch pine, cut one piece 17½ inches long for back of the spice rack.

To make the triangular-shaped top edge on the back, find and mark the center of one short end. Along both long edges, measure and mark 4½ inches down from the same short end. Cut diagonally from the center mark to the marks on the side edges.

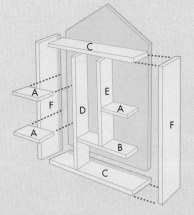

Template Tips

Enlarge or reduce templates as desired on a photocopier. Once the spice rack has been assembled and painted, transfer the templates using artist's transfer paper. You can also decorate your spice rack to match the theme of your room. Use existing motifs as design ideas, or cut shapes from wallpaper or magazines, then decoupage them to the front of the spice rack.

ASSEMBLING A SPICE RACK

1 Mark desired position for two A pieces on piece D. Pre-drill holes, glue and nail A pieces to piece D. Referring to diagram (Before You Begin), repeat steps to attach third A piece and pieces B, E to D.

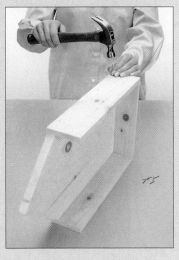

2 Position F pieces along sides of back so bottom edges are flush; pre-drill holes, glue and nail in place. Position bottom piece C between F pieces so all edges are flush; glue and nail in place. Add top C.

3 Positon preattached shelf pieces inside frame; drill holes, then glue and nail insert in place. Fill all nail holes with wood putty and let dry. Sand all edges and wipe off dust.

HANDY HINTS

Customize your spice rack to accommodate bottles in unusual shapes and sizes. Simply measure your bottles, sketch the design on graph paper, then cut the wood to size.

DOLLAR SENSE

While planks are easy to work with, save money by cutting pieces of the same width from one larger board.

4 Beginning on inside of spice rack, paint back and shelves as desired. Apply several coats of paint to ensure all knotholes are covered. Let dry, then paint outside of rack, including edges of shelves.

5 Transfer templates to center of top and sides of spice rack. Using small paintbrush and same paint color as inside, paint outlines of motifs onto spice rack. Fill in shadows and leaf veins as indicated on templates.

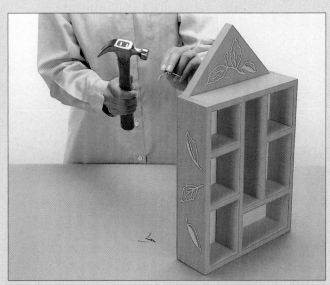

6 To finish, seal paint with two coats of clear-drying varnish. When dry, mark bracket placement on back of rack along top side edges. To hang, position brackets and nail in place.

SIMPLE SHADOWBOX TABLETOP

Protect and display collected treasures in a glass-topped table.

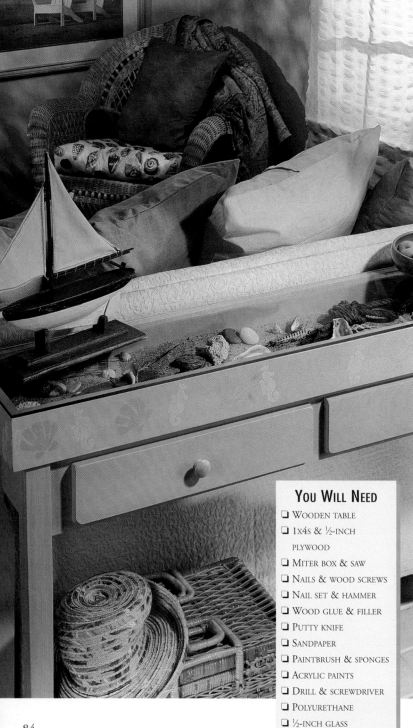

BEFORE YOU BEGIN

Decorate the shadowbox tabletop to complement the contents to be displayed.

Shadowbox Plans

This shadowbox frame is designed to replace the existing tabletop.

If the tabletop cannot be removed easily, cut the frame pieces to fit the top's dimensions and simply place the shadowbox on the existing tabletop.

For the top, have a piece of glass cut at a hardware store to the dimensions of the finished frame top.

Painting the Motifs

To create the ocean motif designs on the side of the frame, enlarge the images (below) on a photocopier to the desired size.

Trace the images onto a sponge and cut around the design.

Practice printing the images on paper before stamping directly onto the wooden frame pieces.

BUILDING A SHADOWBOX FRAME

HANDY HINTS

To increase stability, especially on low tables or in households with small children, use mirror clips to hold the glass in place.

1 Using a miter box and saw, cut four pieces of 1x4 for the sides of the frame. Cut a piece of plywood to fit the inner dimensions of the frame; the frame will surround this base.

2 Using wood glue, attach the miter-cut 1x4 pieces to the plywood base to form the bottom and sides of the shadowbox frame. For extra reinforcement, secure with nails.

3 Using a nail set, countersink all nails. Use a putty knife to fill the holes with wood filler. When wood filler is dry, lightly sand all surfaces smooth.

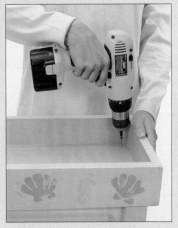

4 Paint the whole piece using a light brown wash (one part paint to one part water). Wipe excess paint with a damp rag. Stamp designs onto frame sides.

5 Paint inside of shadowbox frame light blue and let it dry thoroughly. Brush on two coats of water-based polyurethane, allowing enough drying time after each coat.

6 Set the frame in place on top of table and drill pilot holes in each corner and in a couple spots along the length. Attach frame to table with wood screws.

7 Arrange beachcomber items in frame and affix them with hot glue, if desired, to prevent shifting when table is moved. Pour sand around items. Place a glass top (Before You Begin) on frame.

STAIRCASE DISPLAY SHELF

Create a unique and accessible showcase for favorite books or collectibles.

YOU WILL NEED

- ❑ ¾-INCH-THICK PINE
- ❑ SANDPAPER
- ❑ ¾-INCH-WIDE MOLDING
- ❑ MITER BOX & SAW
- ❑ ¾-INCH-LONG WIRE BRADS & HAMMER
- ❑ DAMP CLOTH
- ❑ WOOD GLUE & PUTTY
- ❑ NO. 4 FINISHING NAILS
- ❑ FOAM BRUSH
- ❑ PRIMER & WOOD STAIN
- ❑ WHITE LATEX PAINT

BEFORE YOU BEGIN

With its tiers of flat shelving, a basic staircase shelf takes advantage of existing space. If needed, vary its size to fit it comfortably beside a bed or sofa.

Maximizing Storage Space

As you plan your staircase book shelf, consider altering the basic design to maximize storage space.

Cut a small, inconspicuous door on one side of the staircase. Add hinges and a small knob, then paint to blend it in with the side.

Instead of nailing the treads to the sides, secure them with small cabinet hinges attached to the risers. This lets you lift the treads and reach items stored inside.

Increase shelf space by cutting the wood treads 4 inches longer and 2 inches wider.

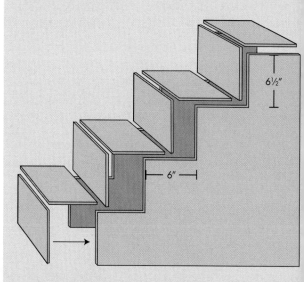

Measuring, Preparing and Cutting

If desired, have all wood pieces cut to size at your lumber supply store. Make certain to have the correct measurements on hand.

From ¾-inch-thick pine, cut one 26- by 11½-inch piece for the back, two 26- by 21½-inch pieces for the sides, four 5¼- by 12-inch pieces for the treads and four 6½- by12-inch pieces for the risers.

Using a pencil, measure and mark placement lines for

the risers and treads at 90° angles along each side piece so the joins form a diagonal zigzag pattern.

Each riser on the staircase should measure 6½ inches high and each tread should measure 6 inches deep (above). Cut along the placement lines with a handsaw.

Sand all the wood pieces smooth along the sides and edges with fine sandpaper.

MAKING A STAIRCASE SHELF

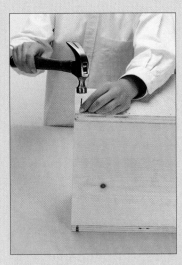

HANDY HINTS

Disguise inexpensive or flawed wood by covering the treads with paint instead of stain. You can also decorate the book shelf with faux paint finishes, cutouts from wallpaper or pretty stencils that match the decor in your room.

1 Cut and prepare shelf pieces (Before You Begin). Using a miter box and saw, measure and cut molding to fit around sides and front of each staircase tread. Align mitered corners of trim, then nail in place to treads with wire brads.

2 Wipe treads with a damp cloth to remove dust. Using a foam brush, paint all sides of each tread, including the trim, with wood stain; let dry. If desired, add another coat of stain to darken the finish.

3 Carefully position back piece of staircase between the side pieces, aligning edges. Glue and nail in place with No. 4 finishing nails.

4 Position one riser on back of each step so that riser sides align with staircase sides. To secure, glue and nail in place. Use a damp cloth to wipe excess glue from staircase.

5 Cover nails with wood putty; let dry, then sand smooth. Use foam brush to apply primer to all sides of staircase. When dry, paint staircase, applying several coats if needed to cover knotholes.

6 Center wood treads so that the sides and front hang evenly over the top of each stair. To finish, glue the stair treads in place with wood glue.

Double-Duty Storage Piece

Build an antiqued chest that works overtime as a coffee table.

YOU WILL NEED

- ❏ Pine boards
- ❏ Latex paints
- ❏ Latex glaze & brushes
- ❏ Hinges
- ❏ Hammer & nail set
- ❏ 4-inch finishing nails & brass tacks
- ❏ Plastic wrap
- ❏ Pencil
- ❏ Ruler & wood putty
- ❏ Sandpaper
- ❏ Painter's masking tape & wood glue
- ❏ Screws & screwdriver
- ❏ 3-inch-diameter ball feet
- ❏ Drill

BEFORE YOU BEGIN

Precut wood helps make this project easy to complete.

Lumber Specs

This project requires 10 pine or plywood boards and four 3-inch-diameter ball feet.

• From ¾-inch-thick wood, cut two pieces 37½ by 18 inches for top and bottom.

• From 1-inch-thick wood, cut two pieces each to these dimensions: 37½ by 12 inches for long sides, 18 by 12 inches for short sides, 37½ by 4 inches for long trim and 18 by 4 inches for short trim.

• Use four shades of brown latex eggshell paint for an antiqued wood effect, and black and gold paints for the ball feet.

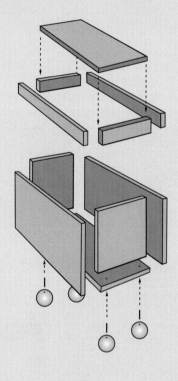

BUILDING A DOUBLE-DUTY CHEST

HANDY HINTS

After the outside dries, paint the inside edges of the lid and the base with the lighter brown. After this dries, wipe on some of the darker brown glaze so that the inside and outside will blend. Treating the inside of the chest is optional.

Using painter's masking tape for freshly painted surfaces is important. Regular masking tape has more adhesive that would lift some of the painted finish when removed.

1 For the lid, place one 37½- by 18-inch board on the work surface. Glue an 18- by 4-inch strip at each short end, with edges even. Glue longer 4-inch-wide strips in place at sides.

2 After glue has dried, reinforce lid joints with nails. Repeat Steps 1 and 2 with remaining pieces of wood to form base of chest. Countersink nails.

3 Fill all nail holes with wood putty and sand them smooth. Sanding by hand or with an electric palm sander, sand edges of entire box to make them slightly rounded.

6 With pencil, mark around the lid ½ inch in from each edge. Press painter's masking tape in place along this line. Partially insert upholstery tacks every ½ inch along tape line. Remove tape and hammer tacks in.

4 Mix each of the three base colors individually with latex glaze. Apply lightest color first. While it is still wet, add two mid-shade colors, blending them with the base.

5 Mix the darkest color with one-quarter glaze; coat one surface of the trunk at a time. Press a large piece of plastic wrap onto the surface and gently move the wrap to create texture. Remove the wrap in one piece.

7 Paint ball feet with gold paint and let dry. Rub feet with a mixture of black paint and latex glaze for an aged look; let dry. Drill pilot holes in bottom of chest and screw in feet.

8 Position hinges at back of chest and lightly mark the openings for the screws with a pencil. Antique-looking wrought-iron hinges or matte brass are good choices. Drill pilot holes for screws and screw hinges in place.

WALL-MOUNTED PLATE RACK

A four-sided oak frame displays favorite plates and cups.

You Will Need

- ❏ 1x4 OAK BOARDS
- ❏ ¾- BY ½-INCH OAK STRIPS
- ❏ CARPENTER'S GLUE
- ❏ NO. 4 FINISHING NAILS & 1-INCH BRADS
- ❏ HAMMER & NAIL SET
- ❏ WOAD PUTTY
- ❏ FINE-GRADE SANDPAPER
- ❏ FOAM PAINTBRUSHES
- ❏ WOOD STAIN
- ❏ POLYURETHANE
- ❏ CUP HOOKS
- ❏ 2 Z-TOOTH PICTURE HANGERS

BEFORE YOU BEGIN

A handsome plate rack couldn't be easier to build. Use it to display your favorite pieces.

Sizing the Shelves

This project creates a rack with a finished width of 48 inches, height of 18 inches and depth of 3½ inches. You may wish to vary the dimensions:

• Consider the number of plates you wish to show. Measure their diameters to determine the size of the rack. Add 3 inches to the height for easy handling, more for hanging cups.

• When suspending cups from hooks, make sure there is enough clearance between the tops of plates and bottoms of the cups so they do not touch.

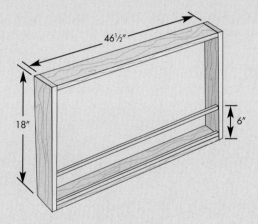

Cutting the Wood

To complete this project you will need two pieces of 1x4 oak cut to 46½-inch lengths for the top and bottom; two pieces of 1x4 oak cut to 18-inch lengths for the sides; and two pieces of ¾- by ½-inch oak strips cut to 46½-inch lengths for the guardrails. Look for oak strips that are straight and without knots.

Attaching the pieces that will form the plate rack frame is a two-step process. First, apply a thin bead of carpenter's glue to the ends of the pieces to be joined. Clamp the pieces together to ensure a secure bond. Allow the glue to dry thoroughly.

Second, reinforce the glued joints with finishing nails. Using a nail set and hammer, countersink the nails just below the board's surface. Fill in the depression with wood putty and allow to dry; sand the wood putty lightly with a fine grade of sandpaper. If the rack will be used to hold heavy plates or platters, make the joints even stronger by attaching L-braces to the corners at the back of the frame.

MAKING A PLATE RACK

1 Following istructions in Before You Begin, cut sides, top and bottom from 1x4 oak; sand cut edges. Attach the two short pieces to the outer ends of the long pieces by joining them with carpenter's glue and finishing nails; clamp to set glue.

2 To form a barrier or kick plate to keep the plates from slipping out of the shelf, attach a narrow oak strip to the bottom shelf with carpenter's glue and brads; set the strip slightly back from the lip of the shelf.

3 To form a guardrail to support the plates, attach the remaining narrow oak strip to the front of the box, 6 inches up from the bottom (or midpoint of the plates) using carpenter's glue and finishing nails.

5 Measure placement for the cup hooks and screw them into the underside of the rack top, with the curves of all the hooks pointing sideways. With the jagged edge facing down, nail Z-tooth picture hangers into the back of the rack on the upper frame piece. Place hangers near corners.

4 Sand the rack with a fine grade of sandpaper. Using a disposable foam brush, apply one or two coats of wood stain, allowing it to dry thoroughly. Add two coats of polyurethane to finish the rack.

CUSTOM PLANK FRAMES

Combine two pieces of wood to create a rustic plank frame.

YOU WILL NEED

- ❑ ½-INCH-THICK LUMBER
- ❑ DRILL & ¼-INCH DRILL BIT
- ❑ COPING SAW
- ❑ ¼-INCH-DIAMETER DOWEL
- ❑ PAINTER'S MASKING TAPE
- ❑ ACRYLIC PAINT
- ❑ PAINTBRUSH
- ❑ STENCIL BRUSH
- ❑ PENCIL
- ❑ SANDPAPER
- ❑ WOOD GLUE & TACKS
- ❑ OAKTAG

BEFORE YOU BEGIN

Transform wood planks into wooden frames. Wood approximately ½ inch thick is best since thinner woods tend to split and thick woods are harder to cut.

Measuring the Frame

Cut two pieces of wood to the desired size of the finished frame. For the back piece, center and draw an opening on one piece of wood. For the front piece, center and draw an opening ¼ inch smaller on all sides than the back piece.

The front piece of wood has a smaller opening so the picture and glass are firmly positioned and don't fall out of place. When the front and back are placed together, a ridge is created for the picture to sit on.

It can be a little difficult to cut the inner opening of the frame to be perfectly symmetrical, but a slightly uneven opening only serves to enhance the frame's rustic appearance.

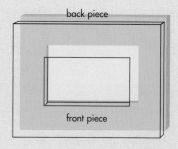

Final Flourishes

Enlarge the template (below) to the desired size. Transfer to oaktag and cut out. Repeat the design three times to create a checkerboard effect.

When the frame is cut, glued together and painted, take it to a glass shop and have a piece of glass cut to fit inside the opening. Cut a piece of cardboard or wood thin enough to fit inside the opening.

For a cardboard backing, cover it with fabric, if desired. For a wooden backing, sand all edges and paint the wood to match the frame. Layer glass, photograph and back of frame and either use a dowel stand or attach a purchased picture hook.

CRAFTING A FRAME

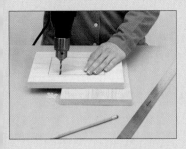

1 Starting from corners of pencil markings (Before You Begin), move 1 inch toward center of frame. Using ¼-inch drill bit, drill holes to allow insertion of coping saw.

2 Remove blade from coping saw, insert through hole and refasten into saw. Cut along each side to corner hole, then cut corner on a curve to next side.

3 Continue cutting away interior until original starting point is reached. Square off interior corner curves. Repeat Steps 1 through 3 on other piece of wood.

HANDY HINTS

For best results, use a dry stencil brush and stencil paints. Dab the brush onto a paper towel before stenciling the frame.

4 Sand openings smooth. Apply wood glue to one side of one frame piece, then lay other piece on top. Clamp in place for a tight seal or weight down with heavy book.

5 When wood glue is completely dry, sand outside edges of frame. Using drill and ¼-inch drill bit, drill a ½-inch-deep hole ¾ inch from bottom edge of frame for 2½-inch-long dowel rod stand. Sand any rough edges of drill hole. Wipe frame and surface free of excess dust.

6 Working on clean surface, apply green colorwash to top and sides of frame using flat paintbrush. Let dry, then paint back of frame and dowel stand.

7 When paint is dry, tape stencil (Before You Begin) along front sides of frame with painter's masking tape; stencil. Let dry, then remove stencil. Insert photo, glass and backing; secure backing in place with tacks. Insert dowel stand.

CONVERTED CABINET FOR DISPLAY

Transform an old cabinet into a unique display case for collectibles.

YOU WILL NEED

❏ SMALL WOOD CABINET
❏ YARDSTICK
❏ PAPER & PENCIL
❏ WOOD GLUE
❏ SANDPAPER & CLOTH
❏ LATEX PAINT
❏ WOOD SEALER
❏ PAINTER'S MASKING TAPE
❏ WATER-BASED VARNISH
❏ SCREWDRIVER

BEFORE YOU BEGIN

Assess the surface damage before giving an old piece of furniture an updated look. Patch and repair any nicks and scratches before painting.

Preparing Wood Surfaces

Sanding concave curves is easier if you wrap sandpaper around a dowel slightly smaller than the curve to be sanded. Place the dowel in the curve and rotate.

Crevices and corners can be sanded effectively with the help of small household objects. Try wrapping sand-paper around a credit card to get into those tight spaces.

To remove a hinge pin that won't budge, use a nail and hammer. Place nail against the bottom of the hinge pin and tap upwards gently until the pin can be pulled out. Wrap the hammer head in fabric to prevent damage.

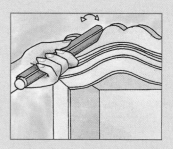

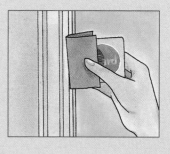

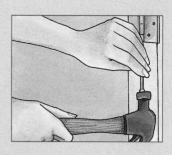

Plan Spacing

Before cutting dividers, assemble the collectibles you want to display.
• Mark off a table space the size of the cabinet. Reposition the display pieces until you find a pleasing arrangement.

• Make sure you have a good mix of large and small items that balance each other overall.
• Measure these areas to determine size and placement of dividers.

CONVERTING THE CABINET

HANDY HINTS

Shelf colors need to work together as a unit. Choose a base color first and then choose other colors with the same value. Paint chips often have six colors; for the shelves, choose colors at the same level on each card.

1 Decide on the placement of the shelf dividers; mark their position on the back wall using a straightedge and pencil. Make sure the dividers create unequal-sized boxes, so you can display a variety of large and small items.

2 Cut the dividers to size and sand the ends to ensure a perfect fit between the shelves. Apply wood glue to the back and side ends; insert the dividers along marking lines. Allow sufficient drying time before adding adjacent dividers.

3 After all the dividers are securely fixed in place, sand the cabinet thoroughly. Seal the wood and lightly sand the cabinet again. Wipe the cabinet with a lint-free cloth to remove any remaining sawdust from all surfaces and corners.

5 When paint has dried, mask along the inner edge of the cabinet front with masking tape. This will help maintain a straight line between the paint colors. Paint the outside of the cabinet; let dry. Remove the masking tape and finish the cabinet with a coat of varnish.

4 Paint the inside of the cabinet using a brush small enough to fit into corners and along short shelf dividers. Keep brush strokes moving in the same direction as the wood grain and work from the top of the cabinet down to the bottom.

SIMPLE RUSTIC PICTURE FRAME

A nautically inspired frame displays summertime memories of the shore.

YOU WILL NEED

- ❏ PINE 2x4S & LATTICE STRIPS
- ❏ CLAMPS & WOOD GLUE
- ❏ ⅜-INCH CORRUGATED FASTENERS & ⅝-INCH BRADS
- ❏ HAMMER & DRILL
- ❏ SANDPAPER
- ❏ PRIMER
- ❏ GREEN & BROWN PAINT
- ❏ PAINTBRUSH
- ❏ ROPE
- ❏ GLASS & CARDBOARD

BEFORE YOU BEGIN

A simple homemade frame can take on a totally different appearance ranging from antique to sleek, depending on the wood and finish you choose.

Choosing Frame Wood

Almost any wood you have around the house can be turned into a rustic frame.

• Pine 2x4s have a chameleon-like quality. They are easy to finish in a multitude of different ways, including the "distressed" finish (upper right) and mahogany-stained finish (right).

• Use unfinished barn door wood for a country style frame that's great for candid photos or fun artwork (lower right).

• To make a 16- by 17-inch rustic picture frame with an 8- by 10-inch opening, you will need two 8-inch lengths and two 17-inch lengths of 2x4 plus two 9-inch lengths and two 13-inch lengths of 1¼-inch lattice.

A Frame of a Different Color

• Paint the frame a bright primary color for a cheery addition to a child's room.
• Soft pastels set off baby pictures or romantic photos.
• Leave wood unfinished to maximize the rustic look. The color of the wood will gradually weather, increasing the character of the frame as it ages.
• Brush on a clear finish—glossy, semigloss or matte—to give the frame a polished appearance that lets wood grain, knots and other attractive, natural features show through.

BUILDING A RUSTIC FRAME

HANDY HINTS

Before assembling frame, lightly sand wood to prevent splinters while you work and to create a smooth finish.

1 Apply glue to ends of 8-inch pieces of wood and attach to inside edges of 17-inch pieces. Clamp in place and let dry. Using a hammer, tap two corrugated fasteners into back of each joint.

2 To make a border to hold glass and picture, on back of frame position lattice strips in ½ inch from center opening. Glue strips in place and let dry. Reinforce strips with ⅝-inch brads.

3 At top of frame's back, use a pencil to mark position of two drilling holes, each 3½ inches in from side and 1½ inches down from top. Using a ½-inch drill bit, drill a hole in each spot.

DOLLAR SENSE

Before visiting the lumberyard, check your workroom or garage for suitable scraps of molding or baseboard that could be used to make a rustic frame.

4 Sand wood lightly; dust with a lint-free cloth. Brush on a coat of wood primer and let dry. Brush on a coat of green latex paint and let dry. Be sure to cover inside edges of frame.

5 Brush brown paint on top of green paint. Apply paint randomly and do not cover all of green paint. Allow brown paint to dry thoroughly before moving on to sanding process.

6 Using sandpaper or electric sander, sand frame roughly in some spots and more gently in others to let green paint show through and give frame a weathered look.

8 Turn frame facedown and set in glass. Place photo or artwork in frame. Cut backing to same size as outer dimension of the lattice inset and attach to lattice with glue or tacks.

7 Thread a length of rope through the holes in the frame from back to front and tie in a large knot in front.

LATTICE INSERT FOR WINDOWS

Geometric patterns add design and dimension to windows.

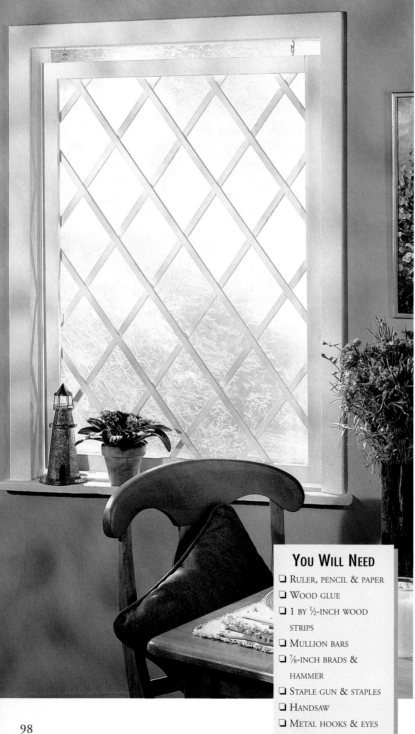

BEFORE YOU BEGIN

Sawing and stapling are the basic skills required to complete this project.

Pattern Play

The lattice insert should fit snugly against the inside of your window frame.
• Measure inside width of window; subtract ½ inch. Measure inside height of window; subtract 2 inches.
• Transfer measurements to paper and cut out to make frame pattern.

• Evenly space mullion bars diagonally over frame pattern. Position lattice design as desired (space bars tightly for privacy; farther apart for more sunlight), then trace lattice design onto paper frame pattern.

For frame, cut 1 by ½-inch wood strips to fit around inside edges of pattern.

Glue top and bottom of frame pieces to insides of side pieces, then nail together with ⅞-inch brads.

MAKING A LATTICE INSERT

HANDY HINTS

To keep the top layer of wood on the mullion bars from peeling and tearing, be sure to use a saw with small teeth, such as a hand-saw. Saws with large teeth will damage wood strips.

TAKE NOTE

When cutting with a saw, be sure to keep your fingers well away from the blade and teeth. For optimum safety, wear protective goggles when using a staple gun and handsaw.

1 Lay pattern (Before You Begin) on flat surface. Beginning on one side and working toward center, align bottom layer of mullion bars. Allow bars to extend 1 inch over pattern at ends.

2 Position top layer of mullion bars over bottom layer as indicated on pattern. Make sure bars are straight and lie flat against each other. Allow bars to overlap pattern 1 inch on ends.

3 Beginning in center, staple top and bottom layers of mullion bars together. Each staple should penetrate wood at intersection. Continue until all bars are joined together.

6 When ends of all bars have been cut, reposition lattice on back of wooden frame. Make sure edges of lattice design are aligned down center of frame. To secure, staple ends of all mullion bars to frame.

4 Position pre-assembled frame (Before You Begin) under lattice so ends overlap frame. Mark cutting lines on bars so cut ends fall along center of frame; remove frame.

5 Using handsaw, follow cutting lines and cut ends of each mullion bar. If needed, hold bars together at closest intersection for support during cutting. For ease, let bars hang over surface during cutting.

7 Paint lattice insert as desired. Screw metal hooks into inside top of window frame, 3 inches in from each top corner. Position lattice insert inside window frame to line up with metal hooks. Using pencil, mark placement for screw eyes at top of frame. Screw metal eyes into frame at placement marks and hang lattice insert by threading eyes onto hooks.

SIMPLE CD STORAGE RACK

Create an attractive unit to organize music disks or CD-roms.

BEFORE YOU BEGIN

A storage rack on an angle adds decorative flair to the storage of square compact discs. Small compartments keep the collection well organized and neat.

Angled and Asymmetrical

Fun and sturdy, this CD storage unit is also efficient.
• The unit is slightly asymmetrical in order to maximize the usable storage space. This form allows nine different areas for storage on its slanted surfaces.

• Paint the CD rack in contrasting colors, such as black and tan, to accentuate the geometric form's shape and style. Or use colors that coordinate with your room's decor.

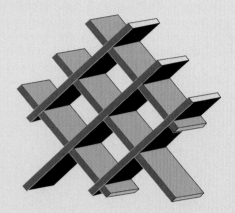

Preparing the Boards

The rack consists of 1x6 pine boards—two long and four short—fitted together in a crisscross pattern.

For the long boards, cut two pieces of 1x6 pine wood to 27-inch lengths.

For the short boards, cut four pieces of 1x6 pine wood to 20¼-inch lengths.

Use a ruler, level and pencil to mark the slots that will be used to assemble the rack.

To mark the points where the slots will end, draw a line across the center of each pine board's length.

To mark where the slots will be, draw a line across the width of each board 4 inches in from the end.

Draw a parallel line ¾ inch away from the first line. Measure out 6 inches from the second line drawn and then again ¾ inch from that measurement; draw lines on these markings.

Draw a third, ¾-inch-wide slot 6 inches away from the fourth line.

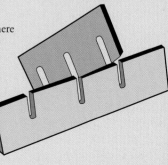

BUILDING A CD STORAGE RACK

1 Using a drill fitted with a ¾-inch bit, drill holes to serve as the end points for the assembly slots on each board. Position the holes along the center line, within each pair of parallel lines that are ¾ inch apart (Before You Begin).

2 Using a handsaw, cut along each line to the drilled hole in the center of each board. Sand lightly, if necessary, to smooth the slots. Prime each board, being careful not to paint inside any of the slots; let dry.

3 Paint the faces of two short boards black and two tan. Paint the faces of one long board black and one tan. When dry, paint all the edges black.

HANDY HINTS

Place a piece of scrap wood under the board being drilled to prevent splitting of the wood along the back side.

QUICK FIX

If the fit between the boards is too tight, sand the inside of the slots until the unit slides together more easily.

If the slots are too loose, add glue to the inside of each slot before positioning the boards.

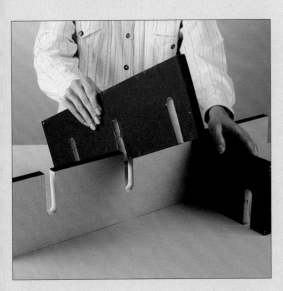

4 To assemble the CD rack, form an "X" with the two long boards by fitting the slots together. Slide the short boards and long boards together into the slots to form a crisscross pattern (Before You Begin).

5 Once together, place the unit on its side. Use a scrap piece of wood to act as a buffer and lightly tap with a hammer to secure the crisscross boards in place.

STATELY PLATE RACK

Useful and unique, this plate rack shows off your favorite dinnerware.

YOU WILL NEED

- ❏ PINE 1x10 BOARDS
- ❏ MOLDING TRIM
- ❏ RULER & PENCIL
- ❏ DRILL & ⅜-INCH BIT
- ❏ WOOD GLUE
- ❏ FINISHING NAILS & HAMMER
- ❏ SANDPAPER
- ❏ MITER BOX & HANDSAW

BEFORE YOU BEGIN

Pine is the best type of wood to use for this project. It's easy to work with and sturdy enough to hold heavy dishware.

Selecting the Wood

Select the best grade of pine for your needs. Varieties range from clear (left) to low grade (right).

Check for clarity, color, consistent texture and a limited number of knots and imperfections.

Cutting the Wood

You will need the following lengths of lumber:
- Two 8-foot clear pine 1x10 boards. (Due to milling, a 1x10 actually measures ¾ by 9½ inches.)
- Three ⅜-inch dowels, each 3 feet long
- Two 1⅜-inch-wide stop moldings, each 6 feet long

Some lumberyards will cut the pieces of lumber for you from 1x10s, or you can cut the wood yourself.

The plate rack (below left) shows the various pieces cut to fit:
- Two pieces for top and bottom, each 24 inches long.
- Two pieces for the sides, each 17 inches long.
- One piece for the shelf, 22½ inches long.
- 18 dowel pieces, each of them 6 inches long.
- Miter the molding after the plate rack is assembled.

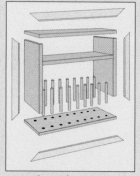

Plate rack in pieces

Completed plate rack

ASSEMBLING THE PLATE RACK

HANDY HINTS

If using unclear or No. 2 pine, prime the wood before painting to hide knots that might otherwise show through the paint.

DOLLAR SENSE

An inexpensive stop collar attached to the drill bit will eliminate guessing when determining the proper depth to drill dowel holes.

1 On side boards, mark a line 6 inches from, and parallel to, one short edge. On bottom board, measure length and mark a dot at center, 1 inch from long edges. Mark four holes 2¼ inches apart from both sides of center dot. Drill holes.

2 On each side board, apply glue to the short, cut edge farthest from the pencil marking. Position bottom board on one glued end, holding boards at right angles. Nail in place. Repeat with other side board.

3 Turn assembly over. Apply glue along short ends of top board. Place top in position, making sure all the edges are square and flush. Nail boards together at each corner and then in the center.

4 Turn assembly on its side and slide shelf into place, positioning above pencil line and making sure edges are flush. Nail boards together. Start all nails so they will center on shelf, then finish nailing.

5 Use medium sandpaper to sand all surfaces of plate rack. Sand both ends of each dowel until rounded. Apply glue to one end of each dowel and insert into hole. Let dry thoroughly so glue will set.

6 Measure each inside edge of plate rack front. Mark inside edge of molding and cut four pieces with 45-degree angles using miter box. Apply glue to molding trim and position along front edge of rack. Tack in place with finishing nails. Finish as desired.

PHOTO DISPLAY FROM CONVERTED WINDOW FRAME

Use paint and family photos to refresh an old window frame.

YOU WILL NEED

- ❏ WINDOW FRAME
- ❏ PROTECTIVE GLOVES
- ❏ RAZOR BLADE PAINT SCRAPER & GLASS CLEANER
- ❏ SANDPAPER
- ❏ PUTTY KNIFE & PUTTY
- ❏ SPONGE BRUSHES
- ❏ PRIMER & PAINT
- ❏ FOAM CORE & PHOTOS
- ❏ DOUBLE-SIDED TAPE
- ❏ HAMMER & ¾-INCH NAILS
- ❏ EYE HOOKS OR PICTURE HANGERS

BEFORE YOU BEGIN

Proper restoration gives new life to dilapidated window frames.

Repair Tips

Wood putty simulates the texture of natural wood.

Place a dab of putty over each hole, then drag the putty knife across the hole to fill with putty.

Once the wood putty has dried, sand it smooth so it blends with the wood surface. Then, sand it with a medium-grade sandpaper.

Once the bulk of the putty has been sanded down, switch to a fine-grade sandpaper to finish the entire frame.

MAKING A WINDOW PICTURE FRAME

1 Position the flat edge of a putty knife between the frame and a piece of molding. Carefully pry apart, scraping away putty as needed. Continue until all molding strips are removed.

2 Wearing protective gloves and using a razor blade paint scraper, remove paint from the glass panes. Then, clean them thoroughly on both sides with purchased glass cleaner.

3 Fill any holes in the frame with wood putty, then wipe excess putty from the surface and sand smooth (Before You Begin). Wipe away dust with a clean, damp cloth.

HANDY HINTS

Many old frames have chipped or broken glass panes. To replace the panes, take a whole pane or the window frame itself into a glass or hardware store and have panes cut to size.

For a decorative finish, have mat board cut to fit the front of the foam core, then position the picture underneath.

4 With a sponge brush, paint primer over the front and back of the window frame until the wood grain disappears. When dry, use a sponge brush to paint the frame the desired color.

5 Cut foam core the same size as panes, then position pictures as desired on the front and secure with double-sided tape. Place frame facedown on a flat surface and replace glass.

TAKE NOTE

Always wear protective gloves when handling panes of glass. Chipped and broken glass are obvious concerns, but even the side edges of a whole pane of glass can be sharp enough to cause serious cuts.

6 Stack picture and foam core facedown on top of glass. Using a hammer, tap ¾-inch nails lightly at an angle around frame edge to secure picture. Evenly space nails around the frame.

7 Attach eye hooks or picture frame hardware to the back of the window frame along the top. Be sure the selected hardware can support the weight of the frame and that the hardware is completely screwed into the back of the frame. With glass cleaner, wipe any dirt or fingerprints from the front of each glass pane.

Photo Display from Converted Window Frame

CUSTOMIZED STORAGE CHEST

Create a personalized chest as special as the treasures it stores.

BEFORE YOU BEGIN

Accurate measurements for wood and fabric ensure a quality finish for your chest.

Making a Tray

• Measure the inside of the chest to determine its length and width. These dimensions are the basis for cutting the eight pieces of wood needed for the tray.
• For the sides, cut pine one quarter to one half the depth of the chest. For the length and width, subtract ¼ inch from the inner chest dimensions.
• For the bottom, cut a piece of plywood to equal the outer tray dimensions.
• Sand the cut wood. With wood glue, glue the sides together to create a frame; secure with brads.
• For the dividers, cut three pieces of pine; one to fit widthwise inside the tray (A), one to fit lengthwise on one side of the tray (B) and one to divide a small compartment in half widthwise (C).
• Make a support for the tray to rest on. Cut ½-inch pine equal to the tray's width to be centered along the chest's inside.

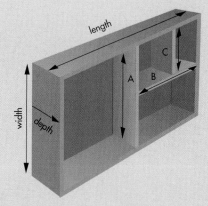

Cutting and Attaching Fabric

Cut the fabric pieces ½ inch larger on all sides than the tray side they will cover. If the fabric edge will be exposed, turn the fabric under ½ inch and press flat. For curves and corners, clip the fabric edges to ensure a cleaner and smoother fit.

Lay the fabric right side down on a flat surface. Coat evenly with spray adhesive. Beginning on one side of the tray, align fabric with wood and press flat, pulling the fabric taut while pressing. To remove bubbles, gently lift the fabric from the wood and smooth flat.

MAKING A DIVIDER TRAY

1 Prepare tray components (Before You Begin). Using wood glue, glue the tray bottom to the bottom of the tray frame. Secure by hammering brads around the edges.

2 Using wood glue, glue two divider pieces together to create a T shape, then secure with brads. Repeat Step 2 with the remaining divider piece.

3 Cut fabric to fit tray (Before You Begin). For sides, spray adhesive on the wrong side of the designated fabric, then fold it around tray edges.

HANDY HINTS

Paint the chest and top edges of the divider before covering with fabric.

TAKE NOTE

Lightweight fabrics such as cotton and chintz are easier to cut and fold than heavier fabrics such as damask and brocade.

4 Repeat Step 3 for long edges and bottom of tray, using designated fabric. Make sure fabric lies smooth and flat against wood.

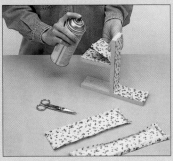

5 To line divider with fabric, press edges of the fabric under, then coat wrong side with spray adhesive. Attach lining to sides of the divider.

6 To make handles, cut two pieces of trim about 10 to 12 inches long. Fold in half and attach one to each side of tray with hot glue. Secure with brads.

DOLLAR SENSE

Look for bargains on wooden chests at unfinished furniture shops and secondhand stores.

7 Follow Step 5 to line inside (two sides and center) of the chest top. When lining the top's center, follow the curve of the wood with your hands.

8 Attach a piece of matching trim around inside edges of top. Be sure that trim doesn't keep the bottom from resting flat on chest.

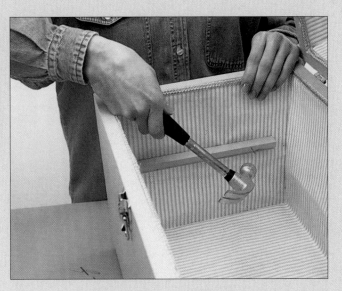

9 Line chest with fabric, then attach wooden tray supports 1 inch deeper than tray depth.

WHIMSICAL WOODEN COATRACK

Fanciful backboards give mundane hooks a decorator's touch.

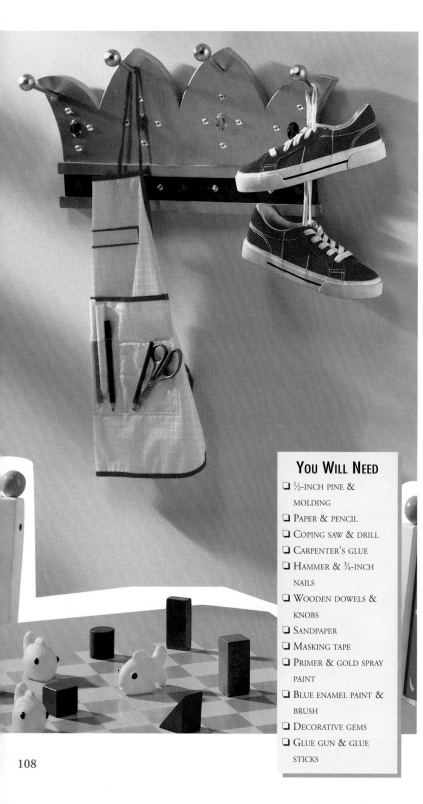

YOU WILL NEED

- ❏ ½-INCH PINE & MOLDING
- ❏ PAPER & PENCIL
- ❏ COPING SAW & DRILL
- ❏ CARPENTER'S GLUE
- ❏ HAMMER & ¾-INCH NAILS
- ❏ WOODEN DOWELS & KNOBS
- ❏ SANDPAPER
- ❏ MASKING TAPE
- ❏ PRIMER & GOLD SPRAY PAINT
- ❏ BLUE ENAMEL PAINT & BRUSH
- ❏ DECORATIVE GEMS
- ❏ GLUE GUN & GLUE STICKS

BEFORE YOU BEGIN

To start, determine the crown coatrack's finished height and width. Cut the pine board to the measurements using a handsaw or coping saw.

Crown Template

To create a pattern for the crown coatrack, enlarge the template (below) to 200% or at the machine's top enlargement. Make successive enlargements until the image reaches the desired size.

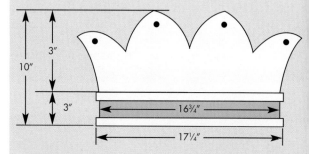

Coping Saw Skills

A coping saw cuts with a thin, flexible, replaceable blade set into a U-shaped frame. Its configuration makes it ideal for hand-cutting curved patterns, such as the crown, especially with soft woods.
• Because the teeth point at an angle, cut with strokes in a single direction rather than a back-and-forth motion.

• For sawing on the push stroke, insert the blade with the teeth facing away from the handle. If cutting with a pull stroke seems more comfortable, reverse the blade.
• Turn the handle to adjust tension on the blade. Too little tension yields a wobbly blade that won't cut straight; too much tension can snap the blade.

Handling Hang-Ups

To mount the completed rack, locate studs in the wall at the desired height and insert two picture hooks. Using two hooks ensures stability when the rack holds unevenly distributed weight.

Screw two eye hooks or nail Z-tooth hooks into the back of the rack, separated by the distance of the studs.

CREATING A WHIMSICAL COATRACK

1 Cut out the paper crown template (Before You Begin) and position it on the pine. Using a pencil and holding the template in place, trace the outline.

2 With a coping saw, cut out the crown. Cut from the top of a point into the corner; back the saw out and cut from the top of the next point into the same corner.

3 Cut two pieces of molding to fit the widest parts of the crown base. Using carpenter's glue and ¾-inch nails, secure the molding to the crown.

HANDY HINTS

Fill in any nail holes and cracks with wood filler to ensure a quality surface.

DOLLAR SENSE

Substitute shiny buttons from the sewing box or beads from a broken necklace for the purchased gems.

4 Mark a spot in the center of each crown point. At each marked point, drill a hole at a slight upward angle for the dowels. Sand the wood as necessary.

5 Cut the dowels to 3-inch lengths. Use carpenter's glue to attach a knob to one end of each dowel, then glue the dowels in place on the crown.

6 Prime the wood; let dry. Mask off the area between the molding strips. Spray paint the crown and let dry. Remove the tape and brush blue paint over area.

7 When the entire painted surface is completely dry, arrange the gems in a decorative pattern on the crown. Mark the design with a pencil. Using hot glue, fasten the gems on the marked design. Once the gems are secured to the crown, the rack is ready to be hung (Before You Begin).

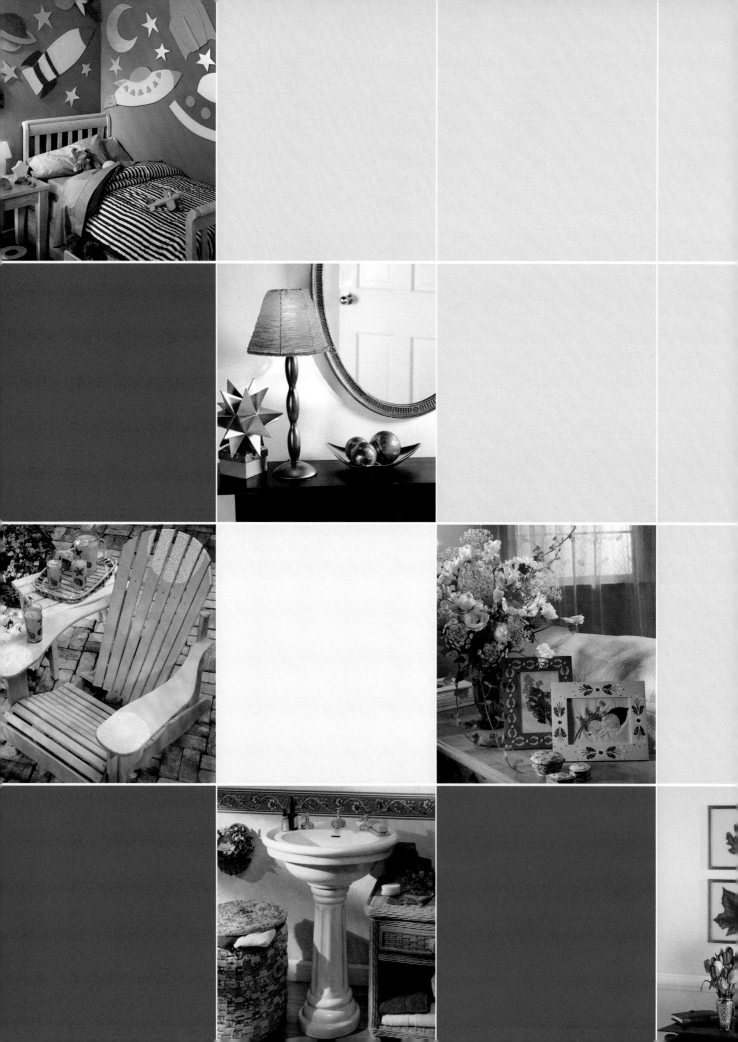

DECORATIVE

CRAFTS

This chapter is full of fun-to-create and beautiful-to-behold home accents you can make with your own hands. We'll guide you every step of the way. Craft a beautiful beaded lamp shade. Coil a cute basket with fabric scraps. Make attractive frames edged with copper foil. Put your skills and talents to good use when you create these wonderful items for yourself, or for giving to friends.

ANTIQUED PRINTS & PHOTOS

Give new photos and prints a vintage appeal with crackling.

YOU WILL NEED

- ❏ PRINT OR PHOTO
- ❏ CRACKLE VARNISH
- ❏ CRACKLE GLAZE
- ❏ PAINTBRUSH
- ❏ ACRYLIC PAINT
- ❏ LATEX GLAZE
- ❏ SOFT CLOTH
- ❏ HAIR DRYER

BEFORE YOU BEGIN

Adding an antiqued look requires nothing more than a water- and glue-based mixture. When coated with paint, the mixture causes a network of fine cracks to appear.

Tips for Antiquing

Combine equal parts of crackle glaze and crackle varnish in a container and mix well. You will need ¼ cup of this mixture to cover an 8- by 10-inch print.

The size of the cracks is dependent on the layer of crackle varnish applied and the drying time. A thin layer of the crackle glaze will create a fine network of cracks, while a thick layer of varnish will create larger cracks. In addition, the longer the drying time between the coats, the smaller the cracks will be.

Choose paint colors according to the desired look. Dark shades of paint applied over the crackled base offer dramatic highlights to the cracks, while light shades produce a more subtle effect.

Once the print is dry, flatten it between heavy books for a few days so the corners don't turn up.

Applying Glaze

Either a bristle paintbrush or a sponge brush can be used to apply glaze over a crackled base.
• Always make sure the crackled base is completely dry before applying glaze.

• Latex glazes work best because they can be thinned with water.
• To remove most of the paint from the brush, dampen a cloth and wipe the surface of the print.

ANTIQUING A PRINT

1 Prepare crackle mixture (Before You Begin). Lay print on clean, flat surface. Using paintbrush, apply crackle mixture to front of print, moving paintbrush horizontally. Air-dry two to three hours, or speed process by drying print with hair dryer.

2 Using paintbrush, apply another coat of crackle mixture to front of print, moving paintbrush across print in vertical direction. Apply even, thin coat to print so crackling effect can occur.

3 When dry, brush only crackle varnish over print. Move brush in direction you want crackling to occur. Crackling effect will begin immediately; do not brush over areas already coated.

HANDY HINTS

In humid climates, allowing the print to air-dry can take up to a week. Dry the print with a hair dryer for a quicker alternative.

An old-fashioned frame and a neutral mat will transform your print into an impressive wall hanging.

TAKE NOTE

Don't brush over an area that is already coated with crackle varnish. This will smudge the print and can remove the crackling effect altogether. Be sure to have enough of the mixture on the brush for a full sweep across the print.

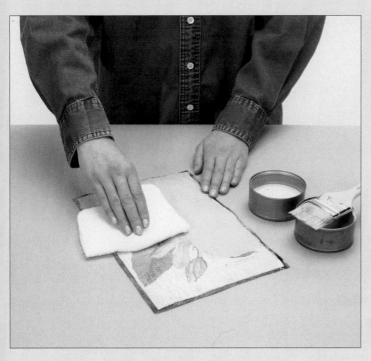

4 When dry, mix equal parts of glaze and paint together; brush over print. Immediately wipe paint from print with soft cloth. Glaze mixture will get caught in cracks, accentuating crackling effect. Allow print to dry thoroughly before framing and hanging.

DELICATE LACE DOILY STENCILING

Stenciling with doilies produces a delicate but long-lasting effect.

YOU WILL NEED

- ❑ LATEX PRIMER
- ❑ LATEX PAINT
- ❑ PAPER DOILIES
- ❑ NEWSPAPER
- ❑ TYPING PAPER
- ❑ ACRYLIC SPRAY PAINT
- ❑ STENCIL ADHESIVE SPRAY
- ❑ 3-INCH BRISTLE
  PAINTBRUSH
- ❑ ¼-INCH ROUND
  PAINTBRUSH
- ❑ POLYURETHANE SEALER

BEFORE YOU BEGIN

Choose the shape of your doily carefully to enhance the furniture and hide any imperfections in the wood.

Choosing Doilies

Consider the overall shape, size and intricacy of the design when selecting a doily.

• Round doilies work well on circular tables, or to provide a delicate accent in the center of each drawer in a dresser.

• Square doilies are perfect for draping over the edges of tables and other pieces of furniture to create a trompe l'oeil (trick of the eye) effect of a real crocheted doily. They can be combined in blocks to create a surprisingly realistic tablecloth.

• Heart-shaped doilies produce a delicate, romantic effect that is perfect for bedrooms or other country-style rooms. They often have the most intricate scalloping along the edges. To emphasize the shape, choose a doily that also features a solid heart-shaped center.

• Narrow strip doilies can be used as borders along ceiling edges and around decorative wall moldings. Choose a band with scallops on both edges, or a border that features one straight and one scalloped edge.

STENCILING WITH DOILIES

HANDY HINTS

Stencil adhesive is a repositionable glue, which means that the doily can be lifted up and moved if you do not place it in the correct position the first time.

Always use a fresh doily for each new position.

1 Apply white primer to entire chair; let dry completely. For appearance of a beige lace doily, apply beige paint to areas of chair where doilies will be positioned. Allow to dry thoroughly between coats.

2 Place a doily facedown on newspaper; spray with stencil adhesive. Position doily on chair. Lay typing paper over doily; press firmly in position. Carefully remove typing paper.

3 Apply two thin coats of spray paint over entire chair, allowing paint to dry between coats. Make sure paint permeates holes of doily. Wear a face mask to avoid breathing in paint fumes.

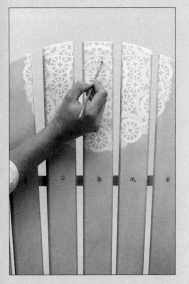

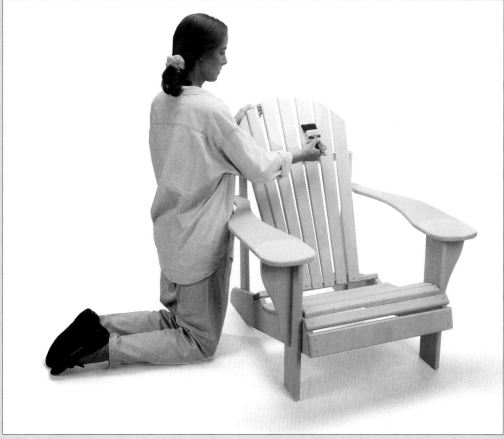

4 When last coat of paint has dried completely, carefully remove doily. Use a small brush to tidy up any parts of design where paint has slipped under doily and created a smudged outline.

5 Repeat Steps 2 through 4 to produce a faux doily on both arms of chair. When touch-up paint is completely dry, apply at least two coats of clear polyurethane to protect chair from dirt and to make cleaning easier.

Delicate Lace Doily Stenciling   115

BEAUTIFULLY BEADED LAMP SHADE

Dress up your surroundings with stunning, original beadwork.

BEFORE YOU BEGIN

Although intricately beaded lamp shades appear difficult to make, beading is actually a simple, versatile and visually exciting craft medium.

The Basics of Beading

Beading is as simple as threading beads onto wire.
• Beads come in all kinds of colors, shapes and sizes (right). Use small, translucent beads for lamp shades to allow light to shine through.
• Standard 24-gauge wire is both strong and pliable, which makes it an ideal base for beading and wrapping.
• Purchase beads in bulk to save money. A 7-inch-tall shade requires 1¼ pounds of beads, or 3,000 total.
• If possible, work in an area where the beads can be contained. Look for a bead tray, or use a tackle box, small bowls or a jewelry tray to sort and contain the beads.

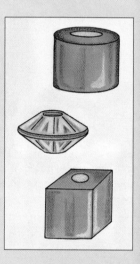

Preparing the Lamp Shade

Select a shade for beading and measure the finished size, including the height from top to bottom (A) and the circumferences of both the top (B) and bottom (C) rings.

Using a craft knife, cut the paper or fabric away from the frame before you begin the beading process.

For shades with bottom rings up to 8 inches in diameter, you will need at least six vertical wire spines to create the best support and shape. Add spines in increments of two for larger shades.

To determine spacing, divide the circumferences of the shade top and bottom by the number of spines. For each spine's length, add 1 to 1½ inches to the height.

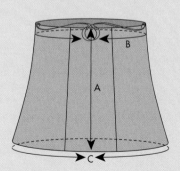

CRAFTING A BEADED LAMP SHADE

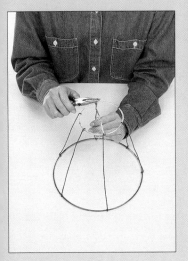

1 Cut six pieces of baling wire to desired length. Wrap end of one wire piece around top of frame to secure; wrap other end of wire around bottom of frame. Repeat to make six spines evenly spaced around shade.

2 Using tape measure and wire snips, measure and cut 2-foot length of 24-gauge wire. To anchor wire for beading, use pliers to wrap one end of wire several times around frame top.

3 Begin threading beads onto wire. Push beads to end of wire so that first bead rests against spine. Continue adding beads until you reach next spine. Wrap wire around spine once, then continue beading.

4 Once top row of beads is finished, wrap wire around last spine to secure. Begin second row by adding beads and continuing to next spine. Always wrap wire around each spine to secure beaded rows.

5 Continue wrapping wire, adding more beads between spines as spacing between them gets wider. To add wire, tie off original wire at nearest spine then secure new length at same point; continue beading.

6 Fill entire shade with rows of beads. To finish lamp shade, add beads to wire, then wrap beaded wire tightly around bottom of frame. At end, twist wire several times around frame to secure; then trim end with wire snips. Reposition shade on lamp base.

Painted Frames with Scandinavian Style

Add a touch of Scandinavia to your home with painted frames.

YOU WILL NEED

- ❏ WOOD PICTURE FRAMES
- ❏ SANDPAPER & CLEAN CLOTH
- ❏ CUTTING BOARD
- ❏ CRAFT KNIFE & PENCIL
- ❏ ASSORTED PAINTS
- ❏ PAINTBRUSHES
- ❏ CARBON PAPER
- ❏ OAKTAG
- ❏ CLEAR VARNISH

BEFORE YOU BEGIN

Achieving the soft look of a Scandinavian design requires little preparation.

Templates

Vary the shape and size of the painted and stenciled designs to fit the frame.

• To ensure balance and proportion, enlarge the designs (bottom) on a photocopier to fit.

• First, sand the frames and wipe them clean with a damp cloth. Then, paint each frame in a different shade of blue.

• Use a hard lead pencil for tracing to create clear, crisp outlines.

• Repeating patterns is a common feature of Scandinavian design.

PAINTING A SCALLOPED FRAME

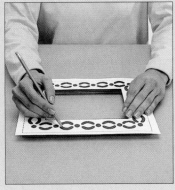

HANDY HINTS

For a muted finish, thin the paint with water before painting the frame and the motifs. Don't thin the paint for highlights.

As an alternative to cutting your own stencils, consider purchasing stencils that feature authentic Scandinavian designs.

1 Lay the template (Before You Begin) on a wooden cutting board. With a craft knife, cut away the inside of the designs to create a stencil. For the circles, press only the tip of the knife into the paper during cutting.

2 Place the template on the frame so the scalloped design is centered. If desired, secure it in place with painter's masking tape. Lightly trace around the inside of the cut-out designs onto the frame.

3 Remove the template. Paint the scallops and circles with medium gray paint and a small paintbrush. Be careful not to smear the design when turning the corners of the frame. Touch up the design, if needed.

PAINTING A FLORAL FRAME

2 Remove the template and carbon paper from the frame. Using a small, flat paintbrush, paint each flower and blossom off-white; let dry. Paint the leaves and flower centers cornflower blue; let dry.

4 Using a small, flat paintbrush, add highlights to the scalloped design on the frame. Keeping the strokes small and thin, add dark gray to the lower left of each scallop and white to the upper right. Finish as described in Step 4 of Painting a Floral Frame (this page).

1 Lay carbon paper facedown on the painted frame. Position the template (Before You Begin) on the frame to center the design. With a pencil, trace over the floral motifs to transfer the designs to the front of the frame.

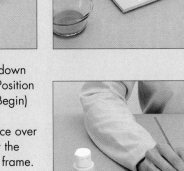

3 With dark yellow paint, paint thin lines for shadows along one side of the flower petals and blossoms. With dark blue paint, add the stems, then paint thin lines for shaded areas to the flower center and leaves.

4 With a fine paintbrush and white paint, add highlights along one side of the leaves, blossoms and flower centers; let dry. Make any final touch-ups, if necessary, then seal the frame with a clear, semigloss varnish. Allow the varnish to dry completely before inserting the desired photo or art and reassembling the frame.

PAPER LAMP SHADE

Create eye-catching lamp shades with decorative paper.

BEFORE YOU BEGIN

Give an old lamp shade new life with decorative paper. For a finishing touch, stencil or stamp designs on plain paper, trim the top and bottom edges of the lamp shade with decorative trim, or thread decorative cords and tassels through the top of the shade.

Removing Old Lamp Shades

Before covering a lamp shade with paper, remove the old shade by running a craft knife along the back seam of the lamp shade. Lift up the cut edge and gently peel it off the frame.

Because the old shade will be used to make a pattern for the new one, tape any rips along the edges and make sure the curved edges of the shade top and bottom are smooth and pressed flat.

Carefully examine the old shade to determine how much overlap existed in the vertical seam; plan to overlap the seam on the new shade by the same amount. Do the same for the top and bottom edges.

To remove rough edges left on the frame by old, residual glue, use an emery board or very fine sandpaper and sand lightly.

Shade Shapes

Lamp shades come in a variety of shapes and can be easily updated to fit a changing decor.
• The cone shape (below top) with one seam will show off a continuous or bold design on the paper.

• The cylinder shape with its straight sides can be covered with striped or bold printed paper.
• The hourglass with flared sides (below bottom) looks best with an allover design to conceal its many seams.

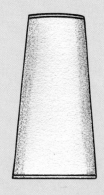

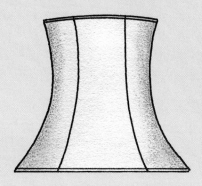

MAKING A PAPER SHADE

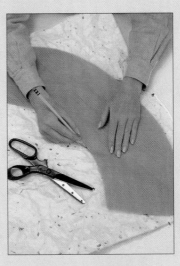

1 Trim rough edges from old lamp shade and measure to make sure shade height is even along entire length. Trace shade on brown paper; add for overlap, if necessary (Before You Begin). Trace pattern; cut out.

2 With both hands, carefully crinkle lightweight, marbleized paper. Begin in one corner and gently bend and fold paper toward opposite corner to create wrinkles. Be careful not to tear paper during process.

3 Gently smooth marbleized paper on work surface. Position brown paper pattern on marbleized paper. Flatten marbleized paper while tracing pattern outline with pencil. Cut out lamp shade.

HANDY HINTS

A variety of decorative papers that can be found at artist's supply stores will be perfect in weight and style for lamp shades.

TAKE NOTE

Use a low watt bulb in the lamp to prevent the bulb from getting too hot near the paper lamp shade cover.

Don't stretch the paper too taut. Removing the crinkles eliminates the decorative effect.

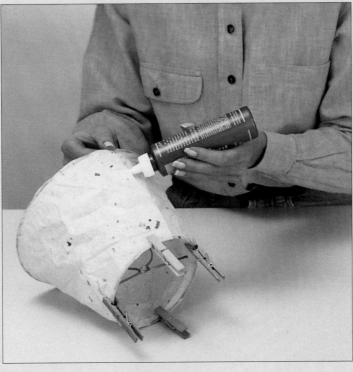

4 Wrap paper around top ring of shade frame and glue along inside edge of ring. Hold shade to ring with clothespins until glue dries. Glue bottom ring to paper, holding with clothespins until glue dries.

5 Overlap edges of vertical seam, glue closed. Hold rings and shade together with clothespins until dry. If adding trim to top or bottom of shade, apply at this time. When glue is dry, attach shade to lamp base.

DIMENSIONAL ART

Take a child's room into the next dimension with imaginative designs.

YOU WILL NEED

- ❏ FOAM BOARD
- ❏ UTILITY KNIFE
- ❏ ACRYLIC PAINTS
- ❏ SPONGE BRUSH
- ❏ MARKER & PENCIL
- ❏ CRAFT GLUE & EPOXY
- ❏ BRADS & HAMMER

BEFORE YOU BEGIN

Any shape or design with simple lines can be turned into dimensional art for your wall. For continuity, choose designs that complement a particular theme.

Template Talk

Use either foam board or plywood to make dimensional art.

Foam board works best when planning large designs—they will be sturdy, yet lightweight for hanging.

Enlarge the templates on a photocopier to the desired size. If needed, you can copy sections of the template, then tape them together to form a complete pattern.

Add extra interest to the display by varying the shapes and sizes of the individual elements.

Photocopy separate templates for the details, enlarging them to the same percentage as the base pieces.

Transfer the templates to the foam board using a marker to trace around each shape.

Design Ideas

Dimensional art is an ideal way to to create a fantasy space. Turn a child's bedroom into an aquarium swimming with tropical fish, a fantasy garden growing oversized flowers or a sunny sky crowded with hot air balloons.

Or, for a more subtle decorating scheme in a kitchen, laundry room or den, make smaller designs to replace a traditional chair rail or ceiling molding.

MAKING DIMENSIONAL ART

1 Lay the first piece of foam board on a protected surface. Using a utility knife, cut out the design following the marker outline (Before You Begin). Trim the foam board edges even. Repeat for each design.

2 Once all pieces are cut out, paint the top and sides of each one as desired, using a sponge brush; let dry. Paint a second coat to completely cover the foam board. Do not paint the back side of the pieces.

3 Lay the detail pieces for each template on top of the base piece. Mark placement by tracing around the corners. Lift the pieces, then apply glue to the base. Press the detail pieces firmly into the glue.

HANDY HINTS

If you're using plywood and you don't have a coping saw, transfer the designs to the wood. Take the plywood to a building supply store and have a professional cut out the shapes.

DOLLAR SENSE

If the shapes you wish to cut out are small, ask building supply and hardware stores for leftover scraps of plywood.

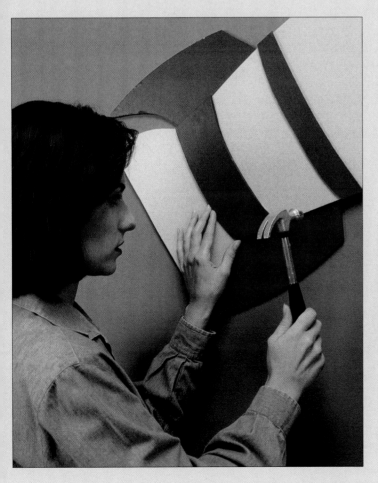

4 Allow glue to dry completely. If necessary, place light weights on top of glued pieces until they are secure. Arrange pieces on wall and use light pencil to mark the placement. Coat the back of each piece of art with epoxy and press against wall. With a hammer, nail small brads around and underneath designs for support until epoxy dries. Remove brads, if desired, and touch up designs with paint as needed.

DECORATIVE WHIPSTITCHED LAMP SHADE

Decorative stitching adds drama to contemporary lamp shades.

YOU WILL NEED

- ❏ LAMP SHADE
- ❏ TAPE MEASURE
- ❏ DECORATIVE PAPER
- ❏ SCISSORS & PENCIL
- ❏ FUSIBLE PAPER BACKING
- ❏ IRON
- ❏ PHOTO ADHESIVE SPRAY
- ❏ HOLE PUNCH
- ❏ SOUTACHE BRAID
- ❏ CREWEL NEEDLE

BEFORE YOU BEGIN

A whipstitch is an easy stitch to master. Simply pull the lacing through the punched hole, over and under the edge of the shade and up through the next hole.

Fabric and Material Options

The new lamp shade paper should be opaque enough to conceal the colors or patterns of the old shade.
• Check to see if a material will disguise an old shade by placing it against the shade and holding them up to a light.
• Choose lightweight fabrics such as cotton, linen or a plain woven blend as ideal materials for covering lamp shades.

• Consider covering lamp shades with some unconventional materials such as wrapping paper, burlap, handmade paper, aluminum sheeting or even woven straw pieces to create an eclectic look.
• Look to colorful shoelaces; natural fibers such as jute, raffia and rope; cording, leather laces or soutache braid as suitable materials to use for whipstitching.

Covering a Shade

For the best results, cover a lamp shade with a continuous piece of paper or fabric.
• Cylindrical and square shades are the simplest to cover.
• To make a pattern, measure the shade from top to bottom edge and the top and bottom circumferences (below).
• The easiest way to cover an odd-shaped shade is to make a pattern for each section, then apply each sepa-

rately to the shade. Or, open the old lamp shade to use as a pattern. Carefully pry the shade apart by its seam and measure across the widest point and from highest to lowest points. This will help determine how large a piece of paper you need to buy. Tape the shade to the paper and trace it.
• To whipstitch either the top or bottom edge of the shade, cut the lacing three times the circumference.

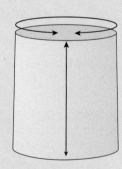

COVERING AND STITCHING A LAMP SHADE

1 Measure circumference of lamp shade, adding 2 inches for side overlap, then measure height of shade (Before You Begin). With pencil and ruler, transfer dimensions to decorative paper and cut out.

2 Cut fusible paper backing to same size as decorative paper. Using iron on low heat setting, fuse backing to wrong side of paper. To avoid burning paper, slide iron in continuous motion over paper.

3 Apply generous coat of photo adhesive spray to paper backing. Wrap paper around shade so edges are aligned and paper is smooth. Continue until shade is covered; overlap paper edges to finish.

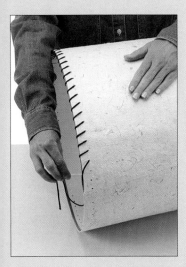

4 Beginning at overlap, mark placement and punch holes at even intervals along edges of shade. Space holes ¾ inch apart and ½ inch from edge for larger shades; space holes closer together for small shades.

5 Thread crewel needle with soutache. Insert soutache from inside through first hole; tie knot. Whipstitch along shade edge. Push needle up through hole, carry needle over edge and up through next hole.

6 Continue whipstitching until back at first hole. Pull needle to inside of shade, then cut end of soutache, leaving 6-inch tail. Knot ends on inside to secure, then cut ends so they are hidden behind shade. Repeat Steps 4 through 6 for other end of lamp shade.

CREATIVE DRAPERY ROD FINIALS

Combine common objects to create finials with an uncommon look.

YOU WILL NEED

- ❏ BAMBOO POLE & ROD HARDWARE
- ❏ WIRE COAT HANGER
- ❏ WIRE CUTTERS
- ❏ 2 4-INCH-WIDE PLASTIC FOAM BALLS
- ❏ SPRAY PAINT
- ❏ UPHOLSTERY TACKS
- ❏ GLUE GUN & GLUE STICKS
- ❏ DRAPERY CLIPS

BEFORE YOU BEGIN

If a window treatment needs a lift, consider changing the hardware. A plastic foam ball overlayed with upholstery tacks appears more expensive than it really is.

Hardware

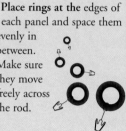

Standard bronze or brass curtain rod mounting brackets and screws are the correct size for a bamboo pole.

9 inches for lightweight fabrics and 6 to 7 inches for heavier fabrics.

Place rings at the edges of each panel and space them evenly in between. Make sure they move freely across the rod.

Each treatment requires varying quantities of rings. Place rings on pinch pleats every 3½ inches, and on pleatless headings every 8 to

Preparing the Rod and Finial

To determine the rod's length, measure the width of the window frame from outside edge to outside edge. Add the width of the brackets, plus 6 to 7 inches for the extensions on each end.

Using a small handsaw, cut a bamboo pole the rod's determined length. Attach

brackets above and outside the window frame, according to the manufacturer's instructions for installation.

To make spray painting the ball easier, use wire cutters to snip a wire coat hanger in the middle of the bottom wire (below). Bend the hanger in half so that the first top section meets the second top section, exposing only one point at the bottom.

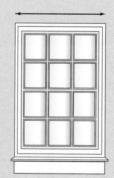

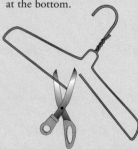

Upholstery Tacks

Upholstery tacks are available in plain metallics or hammered in gold, antique gold, silver or bronze. Other materials such as moss, seeds, push-pins, beads or buttons can be substituted for the upholstery tacks depending on the room's particular decor.

Purchase the tacks from a local upholstery or drapery workroom. These stores buy upholstery tacks in bulk and therefore often sell them for less than the cost at craft or hardware stores.

MAKING A FOAM BALL FINIAL

1 While holding a 4-inch plastic foam ball in one hand, push one end of the bamboo pole into the ball about ½ inch deep. Rotate the ball a few times to make sure the hole in the plastic foam is accurate. Then, remove the rod and set the ball aside. Repeat for the plastic foam ball that will hang at the other end of the rod.

2 Place the cut end of the wire hanger (Before You Begin) into the hole in the plastic foam ball. While holding the hanger in one hand, spray paint the entire surface of the ball using a color that is close to the color of the tacks you are using. This base coat will show through any spaces between the tacks. Repeat for other ball.

3 Allow the paint to dry before adding the upholstery tacks. Press the tacks in place so they are just touching each other without overlapping. Cover the entire surface, except the hole. A 4-inch-diameter ball requires about 150 tacks.

4 With a glue gun, place glue into the hole in the ball and allow it to set for a few minutes. Slide drapery clips onto the bamboo pole. Prop up the pole even with the hole (a few magazines will do), then place the bamboo pole into the hole of the finial and allow it to dry before moving. Repeat for the other end. Attach drapery clips to the top of the curtain.

ATTRACTIVE RAG BASKET HAMPER

Create colorful rag baskets from fabric strips and cording.

BEFORE YOU BEGIN

When making the rag basket, mix and match fabric pieces that coordinate with the room's decor.

Preparing Fabric

Select a variety of fabrics in the desired color scheme. The total yardage necessary for each color or print depends on the size of the basket being made.

For a 21- by 17-inch basket, you will need 15 yards of fabric. Divide the total yardage by the number of fabrics chosen to determine how much yardage of each fabric is necessary.

In addition to purchased fabric, leftover fabric scraps and discarded clothing and linens are perfect sources for fabric strips.

Cutting Fabric and Cord

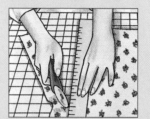

Fold selected fabric in half, wrong sides together, matching selvage edge to selvage edge. Lay fabric on a mat; using a rotary cutter and straightedge, cut 1½-inch-wide fabric strips on the crosswise grain (left).

It may be necessary to join various lengths of cord together. Taper each cord end, starting about 3 to 4 inches from the end (right). Lap the cord ends and wrap them tightly together with masking tape, covering both ends.

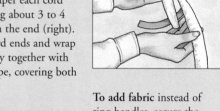

To add fabric instead of ring handles, secure the cord with joining wrap (Step 5) at the starting point of the handle, then wrap the cord for about 6 inches. Form a handle and secure it to the basket with joining wrap (left).

MAKING A RAG HAMPER

1 Thread a fabric strip end through a tapestry needle. About 5 inches from the end of the tapered cord, wrap the unthreaded fabric strip end tightly around the cord, almost to the cord end.

2 Make a loop at the cord end. Wrap the fabric strip securely around both cords leaving a small hole. Continue wrapping the cord for approximately 3 inches. Begin coiling the wrapped cord into a circle.

3 Secure the coiled circle by inserting a tapestry needle into the small center hole, pulling the strip firmly through the hole and wrapping it around the covered coil. Repeat three times.

5 Secure the coiled rows with two joining wraps every 2 to 3 inches. (For joining wrap: insert the needle between the rows of previously wrapped cords and pull the fabric strip firmly through them to hold.) Once a 17-inch-diameter base is complete, build the sides by laying wrapped cords on top of previous rows, securing them with joining wrap every 2 to 3 inches. Continue building coils until the basket is 19 inches tall.

4 Continue wrapping and coiling. Add new fabrics by lapping a new fabric strip over the old, threading the opposite end with the tapestry needle and continuing to wrap the cord.

7 Make a basket lid in the same manner as the hamper base (Steps 1 through 5). To add a knob to the lid, thread a wooden bead onto a fabric strip and secure it to the center of the lid with a knot on the lid's underside. Display the finished hamper at various angles to conceal or reveal the wooden ring handles.

6 Attach a wooden ring on each side with five joining wraps. Finish wrapping the cord. Taper the cord end and wrap it several times, concealing the strip's end.

COPPER FOIL–TRIMMED FRAMES

Create stylish displays with acrylic plastic frames edged in copper foil.

YOU WILL NEED

- ❑ ACRYLIC PLASTIC
- ❑ MATERIALS TO FRAME
- ❑ ½-INCH-WIDE ADHESIVE COPPER FOIL
- ❑ HOOK AND LOOP FASTENER TAPE
- ❑ SCISSORS

BEFORE YOU BEGIN

Acrylic plastic frames won't shatter and are so lightweight that they can be hung with industrial strength hook and loop fastener tape.

Hanging Copper Foil Frames

Once the sizes are determined and the frames cut, plan their hanging placement. Make a template the actual size of each acrylic plastic frame from cardboard or oaktag. Cut out the templates with a craft knife.

Mark the placement of the hook and loop fastener tape (below left) on the cardboard template in the least conspicuous spot, either on top of the foil edging at all four corners or behind the object in the frame, so it does not show.

Use the template to mark the tape placement on the wall and frame. Hot-glue or attach self-adhesive corresponding hook and loop

pieces to the wall and the back of frame. If the tape strip is wider than the copper foil edge, simply cut the tape in half before affixing it to the copper foil.

For a more decorative way to hang the frames, glue inverted picture hanger hooks (below middle) to the upper corners of the frames and string an attractive chain (below right) between the hooks and over decorative hooks on the wall.

As an alternative, drill holes in the upper corners of the frame. Using a coordinating ribbon, twine or decorative cording, thread each end through a hole, and knot. Hang the ribbon over a hook on the wall.

Frame Size

The frame must be large enough to cover the object completely, plus have a border of at least ½ inch and up to 4 inches of clear acrylic plastic on all sides.
• Have the plastic cut to the desired size at a hardware store.

• Clean both sides of acrylic plastic; let dry.
• Center the object on one sheet of plastic and place the second piece on top, sandwiching the object between.

MAKING COPPER FOIL FRAMES

1 Center subject between two clean sheets of acrylic plastic (Before You Begin). Cut strips of copper foil 1½ inches longer than length of each side. Remove paper backing and center first strip over outside edge of one side.

2 Snip tape in half vertically at each end. Fold and finger-press remaining half of tape to back side of glass. Fold first tape end over corner and second end to back. Trim excess tape to reduce bulk.

3 Bind sides of acrylic plastic with foil. Cut additional strips of foil 1½ inches longer than each side. Remove paper backing and place entire width of foil on right side, along edge of two opposite sides. Fold ends to back of frame.

HANDY HINTS

Copper foil is sold at stained glass supply stores and is available in widths from 7⁄32 to ½ inch. Decide the frame size before purchasing foil. To determine the amount of foil needed, double the perimeter of the measurement and add 8 to 10 inches.

For a darker finished edge, lightly rub the copper foil with fine steel wool and then paint it with a tarnishing agent.

OOPS

If the acrylic plastic sheets are slipping during the application of the copper foil, temporarily tape together the sides not being worked on with painter's masking tape.

4 To finish corners at top and bottom edges, use a pencil to draw a miter at each end so that ends line up evenly and smoothly with previously applied strips. Cut miter, remove paper and apply full width of tape to top and bottom edges.

FLORAL
CRAFTS

Whether you use fresh flowers or silk, the bright and natural beauty of the craft projects in this chapter is undeniable. With a few easy-to-get materials and the simple techniques shown here, you can create professional looking floral accents to use as table settings or centerpieces, for hanging on your wall, or for displaying on a shelf of any type. Use these great ideas and add your own creativity to design flower arrangements that you—and your guests—will really appreciate.

SUMMER-INTO-AUTUMN FLORAL WREATH

Carry a little piece of summer into fall with this pretty wreath.

BEFORE YOU BEGIN

Build the wreath in summer using fresh lemon leaves, then allow them to dry and change color naturally as autumn comes around. Choose late summer and early autumn flowers for a true two-season feel.

Choosing Flowers and Foliage

Many dried flowers feature the beautiful reds and pinks of late summer and the warm yellows, golds and oranges of early autumn. Choose from the list below to create your own unique summer-into-autumn wreath.

Pink flowers: strawflowers, hydrangea, roses, statice.

Red flowers: bottlebrush, roses, pom-pom dahlias, strawflowers, celosia, cockscomb.

Orange Flowers: Chinese lanterns, marigolds, statice.

Fresh lemon leaves add a wonderful splash of summer green to a floral wreath. They provide the perfect backdrop for colorful dried flowers and leaves, as well as fresh materials.

After hanging on a wall for a few weeks, fresh lemon leaves dry to a beautiful silver-green color. They will shrink and crinkle slightly, so make sure the wreath is very full to begin with.

Drying Tree Leaves

Dried oak leaves are perfect for an autumnal wreath.
• Always use leaves that are completely dry.
• Leaves are best dried flat. Lay them out on an absorbent surface such as newspaper, cardboard or even wooden floorboards. Leave sufficient space around the leaves to allow air to circulate.
• Dry leaves in a cool, dark room such as a garage.

MAKING THE WREATH

HANDY HINTS

Dried flowers are often very fragile. To make them more sturdy, lightly spray them with hairspray before inserting them into the wreath.

Dried oak leaves can be bought in bunches from floral stores. Sometimes they are bleached a very pale yellow color.

1 Insert sprigs of fresh lemon leaves all around the straw wreath base. Position the sprigs close together and overlap tightly to create a lush, full wreath. If desired, use hot glue to hold the leaves in place.

2 Use florist's tape to make small bunches of oak leaves. Add a dab of hot glue to the stems and insert them into the base. Space the bunches evenly around the wreath.

3 Place a dab of hot glue at the bottom of a sprig of hydrangea and insert the sprig into the wreath. Continue to insert hydrangea all around the wreath, placing sprigs in the spaces left by the oak leaves.

4 Use florist's tape to hold three to five short-stemmed rosebuds. Apply hot glue to bottom of stems and insert them into wreath. Continue to add bunches of rosebuds all around the wreath until it looks full.

SIMPLE MOSS TOPIARIES

Create a variety of simple displays by using moss as a covering.

BEFORE YOU BEGIN

Among the most ancient species of life on earth, mosses are little plants that produce no flowers and have no root systems. But they do have a myriad of decorating uses.

The Nature of Moss

Found from the arctic to the tropics, most mosses grow at ground level at the edge of forests and swamps, thriving in springy, cushion-like colonies. Certain types of moss are used frequently in decorating and can often be found at florist's supply stores in both fresh and dried forms.

Moss is used to hold flowers together, to cover florist's foam or wire, or to add a natural, finishing touch.

Use fresh moss when it is available because it generally has more color and holds together better.

Dried moss tends to be somewhat brown, and it crumbles when handled, though its rustic look can be advantageous in some projects. The following are the most commonly sold mosses:

Sheet moss (below) is green in color and comes in velvety sheets. Use it as a first layer to cover a foam or straw base and to cover containers.

Sphagnum is a tendrilly moss that grows in damp bogs and is valued for its ability to retain large amounts of moisture. Usually grayish in color, it is ideal for supporting flowers and filling wreaths.

Spanish moss (left) is a tree-hanging species and is abundant in the southern parts of the U.S. and the tropics. It is grayish-brown in color and best suited for covering foam.

Reindeer moss, also known as lichen moss, is whitish gray in color and works well on topiaries.

Handling Moss

Moss is fragile and should be handled carefully.
• When gluing moss, use the lower setting on a dual-temperature glue gun. This prevents damaging both the moss and plastic foam.
• When projects call for moistening the moss, don't overdo it; oversaturation can eventually cause rot and discoloration.

MAKING MOSS-COVERED TOPIARIES

1 Cut three blocks of floral foam with a knife to fit the terra-cotta pots. If necessary, taper the foam blocks and trim their corners to ensure a tight fit. The foam should stand about 1 inch above the pot rims.

2 Carefully insert the two-pronged wire legs of one frame, pressing deep into foam until it stands firm. Repeat with second and third topiary forms, using different shapes for variety.

3 Apply thin lines of hot glue to portions of the topiary frame with a glue gun—use one with a low heat setting, if possible. Follow this immediately by pressing small bunches of moss to the hot glue.

4 Cover the entire topiary form, including the stem, with an even layer of moss. Apply a thick layer of moss to cover the floral foam base. Allow to dry for 20 minutes and then snip off any bits of moss that stick out. Dress the topiary with a generous raffia bow.

FRESH FLOWER NAPKIN RINGS

For a well-dressed table, decorate napkins with delicate floral circles.

YOU WILL NEED

❑ FRESH FOLIAGE:
ROSEMARY & IVY
❑ FRESH FLOWERS SUCH AS
BLUEBELLS, STOCKS AND
CORNFLOWERS
❑ FINE-GAUGE FLORIST'S
WIRE & ROSE WIRE
❑ SCISSORS
❑ FLORIST'S TAPE
❑ COTTON BALLS
❑ IRON & SPRAY STARCH

138

BEFORE YOU BEGIN

Grace your table with elegantly folded napkins and fresh flowers. The special finishing touches help make a meal memorable.

Folding Napkins

Fold napkin in half and half again, keeping all edges even. With inside corner nearest you, fold right side corner over so that lower, inside corner is bisected (below left). Fold left side corner over to form point at inside corner, so that upper, unfolded edges are of equal length (below center). If napkins are not creasing sharply, unfold, spray with starch and iron again. Slip napkin ring over lower third of folded napkin to hold elegantly in place (below right).

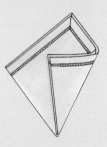  

Napkin and Flower Selection

• Choose flowers that complement the napkins and china. White napkins are suitable for any table setting and any flowers. To create a romantic mood, mix pale pink napkins with pink-toned flowers. For more casual settings, use yellow napkins with the darker yellows and oranges found in nasturtiums and lilies. If fresh flowers are unavailable, work with evergreen foliage for a completely different look.

• Cotton, cotton-blend linen and three-ply paper napkins are the easiest and most elegant napkins to fold. Practice folding the chosen design on paper first.
• Most napkins come in standard sizes; 18-inch, 20-inch and 26-inch square napkins are the easiest to fold into designs.
• When folding napkins, begin with clean, lightly starched napkins and work on a clean, flat surface.
• Store fabric napkins flat to prevent unwanted creases.

MAKING FLORAL NAPKIN RINGS

HANDY HINTS

To prevent soggy napkins, blot excess moisture from napkin rings on paper towel before slipping them onto napkins.

To support delicate flowers, make a small hook in one end of a length of rose wire. Push wire up through stem so that hook lodges invisibly in center of flower.

1 Cut a piece of florist's wire to desired length; twist ends to form a ring. Cover ring with florist's tape. Cut 3-inch sprigs of rosemary; use florist's wire to attach sprigs to ring. Overlap until ring is completely covered.

2 Select several ivy leaves (older ones last longer). Hold one leaf upside down; stitch through and across central vein with rose wire. Gently pull wire ends level; fasten leaf to ring. Group 3 to 4 leaves together.

3 Cut individual flowers off main stem of larger blooms, leaving a short stalk. Wrap a tiny piece of wet cotton ball around end of stalk to keep flower fresh, and then wrap cotton ball with florist's tape to seal.

4 Support stems of bluebells, stocks and cornflowers with rose wire. Position flowers on ring with largest flower in center. Push supporting wires through foliage and bind around ring, keeping wires out of sight.

5 Once main group of flowers is positioned, edge cluster and fill in gaps with bluebells. Mist ring with water and store in refrigerator until just before meal. Repeat to create as many napkin rings as required.

Fresh Flower Napkin Rings

BEAUTIFUL TABLE WREATH

Decorate the party table with a festive, fresh flower wreath.

BEFORE YOU BEGIN

For an elegant wreath such as this, presentation is everything. Make sure you display your center-piece to its best advantage by presenting it in the most decorative manner possible.

Displaying the Table Wreath

A wreath made of fresh greens and flowers could easily stain a tablecloth or scratch a table, so protect the surface by positioning the wreath on some type of base.

Decide whether the base is to be decorative and thus a visible part of the center-piece, or merely functional.
• For a functional, inexpensive base, use a piece of clear plastic cut to the same size as the bottom of the wreath, so that it will be hidden (below).

• To enhance the elegance of the wreath, display it on top of a silver tray (right).

• For a more casual, pretty touch, place the wreath on a decorative platter that matches the china setting (below).

• Raised cake plates, marble cheese plates or wooden cutting boards also make good display bases, as long as they match the table decor. Another option is to cover a piece of cardboard with colored tin foil to match the party decorations.

Floral Perfume

In addition to beauty, flowers add a wonderful aroma to a table setting.

Fragrant roses have a sweet, fruity perfume, although some roses have little or no scent at all.

Irises have a sweet, violet-like scent, particularly in the spring and summer.

Lilies are beautiful spring flowers which produce a rich, spicy aroma.

MAKING THE TABLE WREATH

1 Arrange lemon leaves on wire frame so that leaves cover stems and frame. Allow some leaves to fall toward center, while others fall to outside. Wrap one continuous length of florist's wire around stems to bind them to ring.

2 Wire together small bunches of fresh herbs, such as rosemary, parsley and sage. Nestle bunches, evenly spaced, among lemon leaves, leaving room for flowers to be added later; use florist's wire to hold herbs in place on ring.

3 Trim stems of fresh flowers to a length of 2 to 3 inches, making certain to cut at an angle. Insert stems into small, water-filled florist's vials. New flowers can be inserted into the vials when necessary to add freshness to the table wreath.

4 Tuck flower-filled florist's vials into wreath between bunches of herbs. Position flowers so that colors and shapes are evenly and pleasingly distributed around wreath. Place wreath on some type of base to protect the table (Before You Begin).

Beautiful Table Wreath

HEART OF ROSES CENTERPIECE

Set the stage for romance with this glorious heart of roses.

YOU WILL NEED

- ❏ 9- BY 4- BY 3-INCH OASIS
- ❏ 5-INCH KITCHEN KNIFE
- ❏ GRAPH PAPER, PENCIL & SCISSORS
- ❏ FLORIST'S TAPE
- ❏ FLORIST'S STAKES
- ❏ SMALL SPRAY BOTTLE
- ❏ VARIEGATED IVY
- ❏ 16 FRESH ROSES
- ❏ SEA LAVENDER
- ❏ LEPTOSPERMUM
- ❏ FRENCH WIRED RIBBON

BEFORE YOU BEGIN

Make the heart an even more romantic focal point by displaying it to its best advantage on the table. And when the special day is over, save the roses forever by drying them to use in another pretty arrangement.

Preparing and Arranging the Roses

Use ribbon to give the heart a perfect finishing flourish. Tie a satin ribbon around the heart and finish with a dainty bow. French wired ribbon is another good bet since it holds its shape well.

For a simple yet stunning centerpiece, place heart on a silver tray. In daylight or candlelight, the tray will reflect the ribbon colors and the delicate lines of flowers. Scatter some loose flowers for a romantic country feel.

As an alternative to ribbon, use hot glue to attach individual ivy leaves around the sides of the base, or use florist's picks to hold whole ivy stems in place. Display the heart on a pretty green plate to echo the color of the ivy.

Fresh flowers can be dried easily using silica gel crystals. Half-fill container with crystals, put flower heads in faceup, then cover with more crystals. Leave to dry for two to seven days.

CREATING THE FLORAL HEART

HANDY HINTS

Spritz fresh flowers with water twice a day. Keep the oasis damp but not soaking wet.

1 Cut oasis in half lengthwise to create two blocks that are 9 by 4 by 1½ inches. First, score top of block a few times to determine positioning of cut. Using a 5-inch kitchen knife, cut straight through oasis, using one continuous motion.

2 Place two pieces of oasis side by side. Use knife to shave off any extra to make sides sit evenly. Draw a 7½-inch-wide heart on graph paper; cut out. Pin paper heart to oasis and carefully cut around each half.

3 Stick two halves of heart together with florist's tape. Wrap tape all the way around heart and back onto itself (tape will not adhere to oasis). Cut florist's stake into one 8-inch piece and one 4-inch piece. Push pieces through top and bottom of heart.

5 Cut rose stems 1 inch below flowers; gently insert into oasis to define shape of heart. Fill in spaces with purple sea lavender, and accent with white leptospermum. Soak in warm water and plant food until oasis is completely wet; let drain for 30 minutes. Wrap French wired ribbon around base; drape and twist remaining ribbon on tabletop.

4 Dampen top of oasis heart with a water spritzer to make insertion of flowers and leaves easier. Insert small pieces of ivy over top and sides of oasis. Fill in with more pieces of ivy as shown, leaving much of oasis uncovered.

FLORAL PLACE SETTINGS

Easy-to-create fresh flower arches make your table settings unique.

BEFORE YOU BEGIN

Fresh flowers and greens make any dinner table stylish. For a longer-lasting place setting, use dried flowers instead.

Choosing Flowers and Greens

For a simple, quick arch, wire bunches of leaves together with florist's wire (below). Fresh flowers can also be wired in place.

Delicate white flowers and greens (below) are ideal for romantic wedding table place settings. Snapdragons and daisies look wonderful

on a base of green ferns or other fresh foliage. For even more elegant style, encircle the napkin with matching ribbon and a couple of flowers or leaves from the arrangement.

Beautiful dried flowers (below) make gorgeous place settings that can be used time and time again. Wire together sprigs of silvery dried eucalyptus leaves in an arch shape, then add colorful accents with dried

pink hydrangea and purple delphinium. When they are not in use, carefully wrap arches in tissue paper and store them in boxes in a cool, dark place.

Other Ideas

Use a similar technique to create lots of different variations for the table:
• Make complete wreaths of flowers to encircle a plate.
• Place a delicate, narrow arch between the dinner plate and a charger for a formal, elegant look.
• Use silk flowers instead of fresh for a vibrant arch that will keep its color for years.
• Make small wreaths to match the arches; use them as napkin rings.

MAKING A FLORAL ARCH

1 Stick a self-adhesive mini florist's foam pad onto a round plastic cap; dampen with cold water. Insert one 10-inch spindle stem and one 6-inch stem into either side of the pad, angling the stems downward.

2 Insert two 4-inch stems of eucalyptus or other greens into the sides of the florist's foam; angle stems slightly downward. Cut four rose stems to 3 inches. Insert them into top of florist's foam.

3 Insert four 6-inch larkspur stems into florist's foam; angle stems slightly downward and out toward sides. Fill in any spaces with mixed greens until arch looks full and no foam is visible.

4 Make ribbon loops by wiring together ends of short lengths of thin ribbon. Insert loops into the arrangement between the flowers. Arrangements can be made the morning of your dinner party and will last until evening in damp foam.

BOUNTIFUL PINECONE WREATH

Create a colorful centerpiece with abundant cones, pods and flowers.

BEFORE YOU BEGIN

To dry cones, leave them at room temperature until there is no moisture evident between the cone scales. This process usually takes a few days.

Location, Location, Location

Before creating the wreath, plan where it is to be used and what colors and size will be appropriate.
• For a wall application, a looser, open arrangement built upon a twig base with somewhat ragged edges works beautifully.
• For a table setting, the sturdier, more disciplined wire frame is preferable.

A Wealth of Dried Materials

Cones are scaly, seed-bearing structures that are common to the category of evergreen trees known as conifers. With some 500 varieties to choose from, finding interesting choices (below left) is an easy assignment.

For an interesting mix, combine other dried materials with pinecones. For instance, consider dried artichokes, bundled cinnamon sticks, pepper berries, nigella pods and lotus pods (below right).

Gilding as an Option

The wreath project shown here depends on nature's own tones for its color. If desired, add glittery highlights for festive color.

Hold a can of gold spray paint 12 inches above the cones, moving the can slowly back and forth for even coverage.

Lay out a few sheets of newspaper and place a few pinecones in the center.

Allow the pinecones to dry, turn them over and repeat the spraying process.

CREATING A PINECONE WREATH

1 Cut off the tops of the pitch pinecones with pruning shears. This reveals the next course of woody seeds on the cone arranged in rosette form. Depending on the size of cones, prepare roughly 26 of them.

2 Cut lengths of florist's wire approximately 8 inches long. Using a length of wire for each cone, loop one end of the wire inside the base of the cone. Twist the wire off, holding the remaining 5 inches of the wire free.

3 Wire the cones to the outermost pair of rings on the frame so that each one touches its neighbor and the cones are firmly attached. Repeat the procedure, attaching the cones to the innermost circle.

4 With the two circles of cones secure, glue the smaller, unclipped cones in the middle ring. The pointed tops of this last row will round out the surface of the wreath and add the desired dimension.

5 Decorate the wreath with a selection of unblemished, colorful dried flowers and pods such as yarrow, echinops, peach rose, orange rose, orange safflower, white tallow berry and golden mushroom pod.

LUSH FOLIAGE ARRANGEMENT

Create a variety of lush foliage arrangements all year long.

148

YOU WILL NEED

- ❏ CONTAINER
- ❏ PLASTIC LINER
- ❏ FLORAL FOAM
- ❏ LEMON LEAVES
- ❏ CEDAR LEAVES
- ❏ PITTOSPORUM LEAVES
  (GREEN & VARIEGATED)
- ❏ SEEDED EUCALYPTUS
- ❏ CROTON LEAVES

BEFORE YOU BEGIN

Foliage, available in an amazing variety of colors, textures and shapes, is worthy of its own special arrangement. Search your garden and houseplants for an interesting combination of greens.

Selecting Foliage

Ivy, a popular climbing foliage plant, features leaves in various sizes, shapes and color markings.

Azalea plants, best known for colorful flowers, feature small, oval-shaped leaves that are bright green and shiny. These garden and household plants flower in winter and early spring, but their leaves can be found all year long.

Boxwood, a common evergreen shrub with small, glossy, sometimes variegated leaves, is common foliage in many floral arrangements. The hardy leaves last a long time in water.

Mahonia is an evergreen shrub with glossy, spiky, oval-shaped leaves. The leaves turn almost purplish in winter. Fragrant, yellow flower blossoms give way to blue-black berries in autumn.

Camellia leaves, available all year long, are found on flowering trees and shrubs. These glossy, blackish green leaves have a leathery texture and pointed tips.

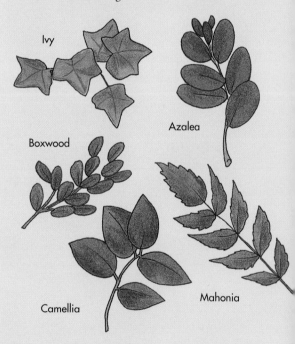

Ivy

Azalea

Boxwood

Camellia

Mahonia

Foliage Types

There are many types of fresh foliage worthy of display. Also consider:
- The variegated varieties of hebe and dogwood.
- Eucalyptus stems in shades of copper, light green or dark green.
- Flowering and berry-producing evergreens like viburnum and holly.
- Sprays of foliage such as rosemary and cypress.
- Unusual leaves like fishtail palm and Bells of Ireland.

ARRANGING FRESH FOLIAGE

1 Select low, open-mouth container with room for cascading of some foliage. Soak floral foam in lukewarm water until thoroughly saturated. Place foam in plastic liner; place into container. Fill liner with water.

2 Work with one type of foliage at a time, beginning with darkest variety. Cut stems of lemon and cedar leaves and green and variegated pittosporum to 4 to 10 inches in length and at an angle.

3 Follow the basic shape of the container when positioning stems. After placing the dark green leaves around the foam, fill in with variegated, flowering and cascading varieties to fill the container.

HANDY HINTS

Soak fresh foliage in lukewarm water for at least two hours before arranging. Remove any leaves that will fall below the waterline in the arrangements.

Revive wilted foliage by putting stems in hot water. After five minutes, add cold water and allow stems to soak for as long as possible before arranging them.

4 Once satisfied with the variety and placement of the various greens, add several croton leaves for color accent. Use them sparingly, but evenly around the arrangement. Change the water every few days and replace wilted or faded leaves as needed.

JAPANESE-STYLE FLORAL ARRANGEMENT

Designers consider Japanese-style arranging a form of sculpting with flowers. It is an art form with tremendous symbolism.

YOU WILL NEED
- ❏ CONTAINER
- ❏ FLORAL SHEARS
- ❏ LONG, SUPPLE BRANCHES
- ❏ SILK APPLE OR DOGWOOD BLOSSOMS
- ❏ HOT GLUE GUN

BEFORE YOU BEGIN

The key to Japanese flower arranging is an asymmetrical display. Stems and branches, which give the illusion of strength and tranquility, are more important than flowers.

Japanese Flower Arranging Principles

Certain plants are traditionally used to create the vertical and horizontal lines that are so fundamental to Japanese design.

Crab apple (1), honeysuckle (2) and dogwood trees (3) provide beautiful blossoms in the spring and supple branches all year.

Fragrant narcissus provide a strong vertical line with their green stems and foliage (4).

Iris blossoms in the winter, spring and summer (5).

Chrysanthemums blossom in the fall in many shapes and warm colors (6).

Arranging with Branches

- Japanese floral arrangements traditionally begin with three main branches set at particular angles to create an interesting dimensional display. Curved lines are used to suggest movement, while straighter branches indicate stability.
- The first branch should be the tallest, about twice the height of the container; in traditional Japanese floral arrangements, it is often shaped like an archer's bow. The second branch should be three-quarters the height of the main branch. The third branch is shorter, symbolizing the earth.
- The container must complement the flowers, foliage and room in which it will be placed. Avoid a very elaborate container that might overpower the arrangement.
- Use heavy metal coils to support branches and hold them at an angle. The branches should not fill the vase opening completely.

MAKING A JAPANESE-STYLE ARRANGEMENT

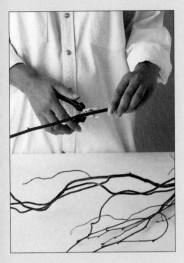

1 Select appropriate number of supple branches or twigs to complement the size of chosen container. Cut branches to desired length based on height of container. Branches should vary in length (Before You Begin).

2 Select a group of different length branches and insert into vase. Manipulate branches to create horizontal and vertical lines. Curved branches are considered feminine and straight ones masculine.

3 Insert more branches to fill gaps in arrangement; do not overfill. Clarity of line is a fundamental aspect of Japanese floral design, so arrange branches to fill space horizontally as well as vertically.

4 Stand back and inspect display. Remove excess branches to keep lines clean. Mouth of container should not appear full. Place a dab of hot glue to center back of silk apple or dogwood blossoms. Position blossoms strategically on branches to add color and elegance to the display.

CASUAL FLOWER ARRANGEMENT

Bring a homey look to any room with loosely bunched flowers.

YOU WILL NEED

❑ CONTAINER
❑ FLORIST'S FOAM
❑ SCISSORS
❑ LEMON LEAF
❑ WAXFLOWERS
❑ GERBERA DAISIES
❑ RANUNCULUS

BEFORE YOU BEGIN

The type of flower, rather than the style and shape of the arrangement, makes the mood of a bouquet. For a casual arrangement, avoid using formal or exotic flowers like roses, lilies, dahlias or orchids.

Basic Guidelines for Arranging

For best results, follow these general guidelines.
• Size: Keep the size of the overall arrangement in scale with the setting. If the arrangement is too big, it will overwhelm the space; if it's too small, it will lose its impact.
• Color: The arrangement's colors should connect the flowers to the room. Cool colors—purple, blue and white—look serene and restful. Warm colors—red, orange and pink—are more lively.
• Containers: Choose a plain and simple container such as earthenware, pottery, clear glass or milk glass.

For a triangular shape, use open-petaled flowers such as daisies, chrysanthemums, sunflowers and black-eyed Susans as the primary focus.

For a round arrangement (below top), choose flowers with large, round blooms like geraniums, hydrangea, zinnias, peonies and marigolds.

For a fan-shaped bouquet (below bottom), arrange spiky, linear flowers such as lavender, delphinium, larkspur, snapdragons, liatris and stock.

MAKING A CASUAL BOUQUET

1 Cut florist's foam to fit snugly inside container; fill about halfway with water. Cut about four or five lemon leaf stems and push them into foam around outer edge of the container.

2 Take waxflower stems and break off several small stalks. Position them in the space left inside the outer border of lemon leaves. Remove any lower flowers and foliage that will fall below the waterline.

3 Place one tall yellow gerbera daisy in the center of the arrangement. Continue working your way down, positioning daisies on either side and in front to form a loose triangular-shaped arrangement.

HANDY HINTS

If arranging in a clear glass vase, surround a small block of florist's foam with clear glass marbles. Or omit florist's foam and use marbles only.

4 Fill out triangular shape with the orange ranunculus. Position four or five blossoms to add splashes of color, turning the vase to be sure the color is scattered throughout. Stand back from the arrangement to find any open areas and blank spots. Fill these with extra waxflowers. Fill the container with water and position for display.

INSTANT IVY TOPIARY

Create striking topiaries almost instantly with quick-growing ivy.

BEFORE YOU BEGIN

Ivy is the symbol of happiness and fidelity. With proper care, a beautiful ivy topiary can provide years of enjoyment in almost any room in the house.

The Right Lighting

• Ivy topiaries can be kept in bright light or shady locations. The variegated species of ivy tend to keep their color better in brighter conditions, but some varieties can tolerate very low levels of light.

• The topiary will maintain good color and remain compact if the lighting is just right for that particular species of ivy.

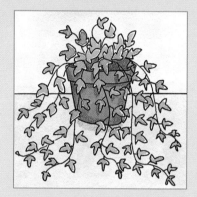

Caring for the Plant

Choose an ivy plant with lots of long trails (above) that are at least 2 feet long.

Keep the soil slightly moist. Generally, ivy plants don't care for a lot of water or dry soil for prolonged periods. Water more frequently in spring and fall.

Ivy will thrive if the temperature ranges between 65° and 85°F. Some ivy can withstand almost freezing outdoor temperatures, but it is better to bring the plant in until frost has passed.

During spring and summer months, feed the plant with a liquid houseplant fertilizer every other watering. Avoid fertilizing during the winter months.

Further Care

Keep the topiary in good shape by winding any new growth around the topiary form and pulling out dry leaves. Prune the plant regularly to maintain its unique shape. Pinch long shoots so the plant remains full and compact.

To avoid infestation by spider mites, which are common pests to ivies, spray regularly with an insect spray. Contact your local nursery for specific advice.

PREPARING PLANT MATERIAL

1 Plant the ivy in a terra-cotta pot filled with potting soil. Make certain that the ivy is planted firmly. The ivy plant should have at least 2-foot-long trails (or should be allowed to grow) to begin creating a topiary form.

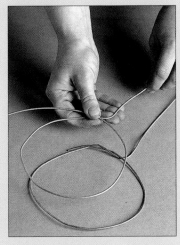

2 For a globe-shaped topiary, cut two 29-inch-long pieces of wire. Make two lollipop shapes using a twisting motion to form a circle at one end of each wire. Secure by twisting the ends of the wire together.

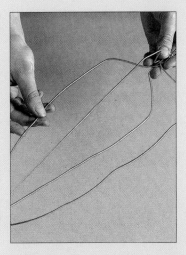

3 The same basic idea can be used to form a variety of different topiaries. One variation is the Christmas tree shape, created by making triangle shapes instead of lollipops out of two 41-inch-long pieces of wire.

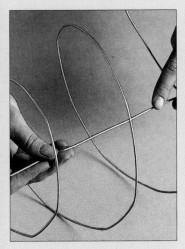

4 For a spiral topiary, first cut a 100-inch piece of wire. The 15-inch central post should be created before the coils. Form the coils around the central post. Secure the end of last spiral by twisting it around the central post.

5 To finish a sphere (Step 2), join the two lollipop shapes by placing one inside the other. Twist the two stems together to secure. You may further reinforce the sphere by wrapping another piece of wire around the stems.

6 Place the topiary frame in the middle of the prepared pot and spread the ivy trails. Working from bottom to top, wind the ivy around the wire frame and gently tie the ivy to the frame, covering as much wire as possible. Use galvanized wire pins to anchor the base firmly.

DRIED FLOWER GARDEN BOX

Arrange dried flowers in levels to create an everlasting flower box.

YOU WILL NEED
- ❏ Straw basket
- ❏ Florist's foam
- ❏ Glue gun & glue sticks
- ❏ Green sheet moss
- ❏ Briza, larkspur, amaranthus, peony, timothy, nigella orientalis
- ❏ Grape clusters
- ❏ Florist's scissors

BEFORE YOU BEGIN

To make a vertical arrangement, choose flowers and grasses that feature long, full stems that stand firmly upright, rather than flower heads with bare stems.

Choosing Dried Flowers

For this vertical arrangement, prepare the dried flowers by grouping like flowers into clusters and trimming the stems to predetermined lengths. When cutting the stems, keep in mind that they will be pushed 2 inches into the florist's foam. Trim stems on an angle—this will make inserting them into foam easier.

Larkspur is a colorful, spike-like flower with a long, full stem (1). Divide the larkspur into small clusters by color (pink, white and blue). Cut the stems of the pink larkspur to 18 inches and the white stems to 15 inches. Divide the blue larkspur into two clusters, one 8 inches and one 15 inches.

Amaranthus, also called love-lies-bleeding, resembles a long rope of crimson flowers (2). Divide into clusters and trim the stems to 23 inches and 12 inches.

Briza is a grass with compact heads that resemble puffed rice (3). Cut two separate clusters; 25 inches and 12 inches long.

Timothy is a rat-tail grass (4). Any other cream-tinted grass, such as seteria, that features a long, fluffy head is a suitable substitute. Cut two clusters, 11 inches and 9 inches long.

Nigella orientalis is a spiked seedhead (5). Cut it short to fill in the base of the arrangement. Cut the stems in varying lengths ranging from 1 inch to 5 inches.

Peonies are big, beautiful and bold flowers (6). Cut the stems of two large heads to lengths of 5 inches and 6 inches.

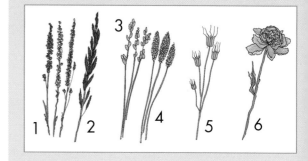

CREATING A GARDEN BOX

1 Cut florist's foam to fit snugly in the basket. Secure foam to basket with a few drops of hot glue on bottom of foam. Tuck sheet moss between foam and basket sides to fill gap.

2 Gather up clumps of precut flowers, beginning with briza, which are the tallest stems. Push stems into foam at back of arrangement. Add pink larkspur to side of briza.

4 Fill in gaps around front and sides of the arrangement with nigella pods and peony heads. Insert two or three clusters of artificial grapes in one corner of the basket.

3 Continue adding clusters of flowers to the arrangement according to size. Place tallest stems at the back and work toward the front.

Index